Maker Innovations Series

Jump start your path to discovery with the Apress Maker Innovations series! From the basics of electricity and components through to the most advanced options in robotics and Machine Learning, you'll forge a path to building ingenious hardware and controlling it with cutting-edge software. All while gaining new skills and experience with common toolsets you can take to new projects or even into a whole new career.

The Apress Maker Innovations series offers projects-based learning, while keeping theory and best processes front and center. So you get hands-on experience while also learning the terms of the trade and how entrepreneurs, inventors, and engineers think through creating and executing hardware projects. You can learn to design circuits, program AI, create IoT systems for your home or even city, and so much more!

Whether you're a beginning hobbyist or a seasoned entrepreneur working out of your basement or garage, you'll scale up your skillset to become a hardware design and engineering pro. And often using low-cost and open-source software such as the Raspberry Pi, Arduino, PIC microcontroller, and Robot Operating System (ROS). Programmers and software engineers have great opportunities to learn, too, as many projects and control environments are based in popular languages and operating systems, such as Python and Linux.

If you want to build a robot, set up a smart home, tackle assembling a weather-ready meteorology system, or create a brand-new circuit using breadboards and circuit design software, this series has all that and more! Written by creative and seasoned Makers, every book in the series tackles both tested and leading-edge approaches and technologies for bringing your visions and projects to life.

More information about this series at https://link.springer.com/bookseries/17311

Essentials of Arduino™ Boards Programming

Step-by-Step Guide to Master Arduino Boards Hardware and Software

Farzin Asadi

Apress®

Essentials of Arduino™ Boards Programming: Step-by-Step Guide to Master Arduino Boards Hardware and Software

Farzin Asadi
Department of Electrical and Electronics Engineering, Maltepe University,
Istanbul, Türkiye

ISBN-13 (pbk): 978-1-4842-9599-1   ISBN-13 (electronic): 978-1-4842-9600-4
https://doi.org/10.1007/978-1-4842-9600-4

Copyright © 2023 by Farzin Asadi

Managing Director, Apress Media LLC: Welmoed Spahr
Acquisitions Editor: Miriam Haidara
Development Editor: James Markham
Coordinating Editor: Jessica Vakili

Cover image designed by eStudioCalamar

Distributed to the book trade worldwide by Apress Media, LLC, 1 New York Plaza, New York, NY 10004, U.S.A. Phone 1-800-SPRINGER, fax (201) 348-4505, e-mail orders-ny@springer-sbm.com, or visit www.springeronline.com. Apress Media, LLC is a California LLC and the sole member (owner) is Springer Science + Business Media Finance Inc (SSBM Finance Inc). SSBM Finance Inc is a **Delaware** corporation.

For information on translations, please e-mail booktranslations@springernature.com; for reprint, paperback, or audio rights, please e-mail bookpermissions@springernature.com.

Apress titles may be purchased in bulk for academic, corporate, or promotional use. eBook versions and licenses are also available for most titles. For more information, reference our Print and eBook Bulk Sales web page at http://www.apress.com/bulk-sales.

Any source code or other supplementary material referenced by the author in this book is available to readers on GitHub (https://github.com/Apress). For more detailed information, please visit http://www.apress.com/source-code.

Paper in this product is recyclable

Dedicated to my lovely brother, Farzad, and my lovely sisters, Farnaz and Farzaneh.

Table of Contents

About the Author

Farzin Asadi received his BSc in Electronics Engineering, MSc in Control Engineering, and PhD in Mechatronics Engineering.

Currently, he is with the Department of Electrical and Electronics Engineering at Maltepe University, Istanbul, Turkey.

Dr. Asadi has published more than 40 papers in ISI/Scopus indexed journals. He has written 25 books. His research interests include switching converters, control theory, robust control of power electronics converters, and robotics.

About the Technical Reviewer

Hai Van Pham received his BSc, MSc, and PhD in Computer Science.

Currently, he is with the School of Information and Communication Technology, Hanoi University of Science and Technology, Hanoi, Vietnam.

Dr. Pham has published over 100 papers in ISI/Scopus indexed journals. He is an associate editor in domestic and international journals and served as chair and technical committee member of many national and international conferences including SOICT 2014, KSE 2015, KSE 2017, KSE 2019, KSE 2021, and KSE 2022.

His research interests include artificial intelligence, knowledge-based systems, big data, soft computing, rule-based systems, and fuzzy systems.

Introduction

Arduino is an open source hardware and software company, project, and user community that designs and manufactures single-board microcontrollers and microcontroller kits for building digital devices.

Arduino boards use a variety of microcontrollers, and each board is suitable for a specific application. For instance, Arduino Nano or Pro Mini is an ideal option if space or weight is important for you. If you search for a board with many input/output (I/O) pins, then Arduino MEGA is a good option for you. If you need an Arduino board for a time-critical application like a robot control, then Arduino DUE is a good choice. Arduino UNO is a good option for educational purposes. All of the examples in this book are done with Arduino UNO.

There exist many other development boards in the world, but why are Arduino boards so famous with millions of users? Here are some of the basic reasons that make Arduino boards outstanding:

1) Arduino has an official free of charge Integrated Development Environment (IDE) to make coding easier, especially for beginners. The Arduino IDE has a minimalist interface, making it simple to write, compile, and upload the code to the Arduino board. It is a versatile software compatible with Windows, Linux, and macOS.

2) The Arduino IDE is also preloaded with a broad library of codes that users can use, modify, or practice. Users can use these codes instead of coding from scratch or can modify the codes for

similar projects. This makes learning easier for beginners because they already have codes to familiarize themselves with, along with tons of tutorials from Arduino's community. It also benefits professionals by saving them time because they can simply copy nuggets of codes that they need for their projects from the libraries.

3) Programming an Arduino board requires no external programmer. All you need is a USB cable to connect your Arduino board to the computer.

4) Many types of shields are designed for Arduino boards. Shields are modular circuit boards that piggyback onto the Arduino board to instill it with extra functionality.

Therefore, enough reasons for learning how to work with Arduino boards exist!

This book is for Arduino enthusiasts of all experience levels. Being familiar with a programming language (especially C) is an advantage; however, it is not necessary. This book is full of solved examples. All of the given examples are tested. In many cases, you can edit the given codes to solve your own problems.

This book is composed of 11 chapters. Here is a brief summary of each chapter:

Chapter 1 is an introductory chapter about microcontrollers and Arduino boards.

Chapter 2 shows how to generate or read digital data.

Chapter 3 shows how to generate and read analog data.

Chapter 4 shows how to connect a Liquid Crystal Display (LCD) or an Electrically Erasable Programmable Read-Only Memory (EEPROM) to an Arduino board.

Chapter 5 shows how to use serial communication to transfer data between an Arduino board and a computer.

Chapter 6 introduces the ready-to-use mathematical functions available in the Arduino IDE.

Chapter 7 shows how to generate a pulse width modulation (PWM) signal with an Arduino board.

Chapter 8 shows how different types of motors can be controlled with an Arduino board.

Chapter 9 introduces the interrupts and shows how to use them.

Chapter 10 introduces the timers and shows how timers can be programmed in Clear Timer on Compare Match (CTC) mode.

Chapter 11 shows how different types of sensors can be read with an Arduino board.

I hope that this book will be useful to the readers, and I welcome comments on the book.

CHAPTER 1

Introduction to Arduino Boards

1.1 Introduction

Arduino is an open source platform used for building electronics projects. Arduino consists of both a physical programmable circuit board (often referred to as a microcontroller) and a piece of software or IDE (Integrated Development Environment) that runs on your computer, used to write and upload computer code to the physical board.

The Arduino platform has become quite popular with people just starting out with electronics, and for good reason. Unlike most previous programmable circuit boards, the Arduino does not need a separate piece of hardware (called a programmer) in order to load new code onto the board; you can simply use a USB cable. Additionally, the Arduino IDE uses a simplified version of C++, making it easier to learn to program. Finally, Arduino provides a standard form factor that breaks out the functions of the microcontroller into a more accessible package.

This chapter is an introduction to microcontrollers and Arduino boards and makes the foundation for other chapters.

© Farzin Asadi 2023
F. Asadi, *Essentials of Arduino™ Boards Programming*, Maker Innovations Series,
https://doi.org/10.1007/978-1-4842-9600-4_1

1.2 Microcontrollers

A microcontroller is a compact integrated circuit designed to govern a specific operation in an embedded system. A typical microcontroller includes a processor, memory, and input/output (I/O) peripherals on a single chip. Some of the commonly used microcontrollers are shown in Figures 1-1 to 1-3.

Figure 1-1. *A microcontroller made by ATMEL*

Figure 1-2. *A microcontroller made by Microchip*

Figure 1-3. *A microcontroller made by STMicroelectronics*

Sometimes referred to as an embedded controller or microcontroller unit (MCU), microcontrollers are found in vehicles, robots, office machines, medical devices, mobile radio transceivers, vending machines, and home appliances, among other devices. They are essentially simple miniature personal computers (PCs) designed to control small features of a larger component, without a complex front-end operating system (OS).

For example, a car might have many microcontrollers that control various individual systems within, such as the antilock braking system, traction control, fuel injection, or suspension control. All the microcontrollers communicate with each other to inform the correct actions. Some might communicate with a more complex central computer within the car, and others might only communicate with other microcontrollers. They send and receive data using their I/O peripherals and process that data to perform their designated tasks.

1.3 Elements of a Microcontroller

The core elements of a microcontroller are

The processor (CPU): A processor can be thought
of as the brain of the device. It processes and
responds to various instructions that direct the
microcontroller's function. This involves performing
basic arithmetic, logic, and I/O operations. It
also performs data transfer operations, which
communicate commands to other components in
the larger embedded system.

Memory: A microcontroller's memory is used to
store the data that the processor receives and uses to
respond to instructions that it's been programmed
to carry out. A microcontroller has two main
memory types: program memory and data memory.

Program memory stores long-term information about the instructions
that the CPU carries out. Program memory is nonvolatile memory,
meaning it holds information over time without needing a power source.

Data memory is required for temporary data storage while the
instructions are being executed. Data memory is volatile, meaning the data
it holds is temporary and is only maintained if the device is connected to a
power source.

I/O peripherals: The input and output devices are
the interface for the processor to the outside world.
The input ports receive information and send it
to the processor in the form of binary data. The
processor receives that data and sends the necessary
instructions to output devices that execute tasks
external to the microcontroller.

While the processor, memory, and I/O peripherals are the defining elements of the microprocessor, there are other elements that are frequently included. The term I/O peripherals itself simply refers to supporting components that interface with the memory and processor. There are many supporting components that can be classified as peripherals. Having some manifestation of an I/O peripheral is elemental to a microprocessor, because they are the mechanism through which the processor is applied.

Other supporting elements of a microcontroller include

> **Analog-to-digital converter (ADC)**: An ADC is a circuit that converts analog signals to digital signals. It allows the processor at the center of the microcontroller to interface with external analog devices, such as sensors.

> **Digital-to-analog converter (DAC)**: A DAC performs the inverse function of an ADC and allows the processor at the center of the microcontroller to communicate its outgoing signals to external analog components.

> **System bus**: The system bus is the connective wire that links all components of the microcontroller together.

> **Serial port**: The serial port is one example of an I/O port that allows the microcontroller to connect to external components. It has a similar function to a USB or a parallel port but differs in the way it exchanges bits.

1.4 Difference Between Microcontroller and Microprocessor

The distinction between microcontrollers and microprocessors has gotten less clear as chip density and complexity have become relatively cheap to manufacture, and microcontrollers have thus integrated more "general computer" types of functionality. On the whole, though, microcontrollers can be said to function usefully on their own, with a direct connection to sensors and actuators, where microprocessors are designed to maximize compute power on the chip, with internal bus connections (rather than direct I/O) to supporting hardware such as RAM and serial ports. Simply put, coffee makers use microcontrollers; desktop computers use microprocessors.

Microcontrollers are less expensive and use less power than microprocessors. Microprocessors do not have built-in RAM, read-only memory (ROM), or other peripherals on the chip, but rather attach to these with their pins. A microprocessor can be considered the heart of a computer system, whereas a microcontroller can be considered the heart of an embedded system.

1.5 Arduino Boards

In a nutshell, an Arduino (/ɑːrˈdwiːnoʊ/) is an open hardware development board that can be used by tinkerers, hobbyists, and makers to design and build devices that interact with the real world.

The Arduino hardware and software were designed for artists, designers, hobbyists, hackers, newbies, and anyone interested in creating interactive objects or environments. Arduino can interact with buttons, LEDs, motors, speakers, GPS units, cameras, the Internet, and even your smartphone or your TV! This flexibility combined with the fact that the Arduino software is free, the hardware boards are pretty cheap, and both the software and hardware are easy to learn has led to a large community of users who have contributed code and released instructions for a huge variety of Arduino-based projects.

Most Arduino boards use Atmel 8-bit microcontrollers (ATmega8, ATmega168, ATmega328, ATmega1280, or ATmega2560). Some Arduino boards use ARM Cortex–based microcontrollers.

Some of the commonly used Arduino boards are shown in Figures 1-4 to 1-6.

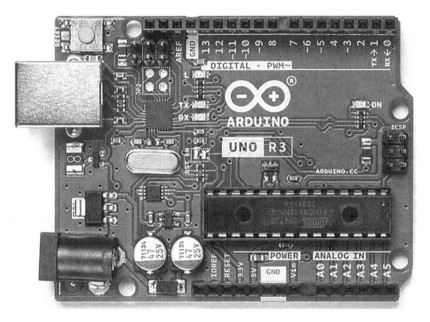

Figure 1-4. *Arduino UNO board*

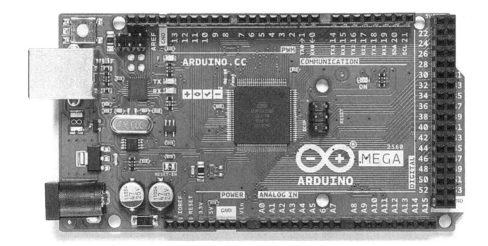

Figure 1-5. *Arduino MEGA board*

Figure 1-6. *Arduino Nano board*

All of the experiments of this book are done with the aid of the Arduino UNO board (Figure 1-4). Arduino UNO uses the ATmega328 microcontroller made by ATMEL. ATmega328 is made in different packages (Figures 1-7 and 1-8).

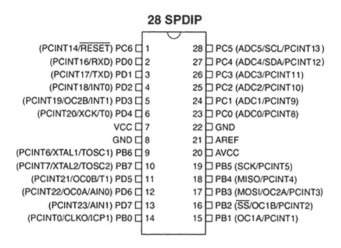

Figure 1-7. *Dual inline package (DIP) version of ATmega328*

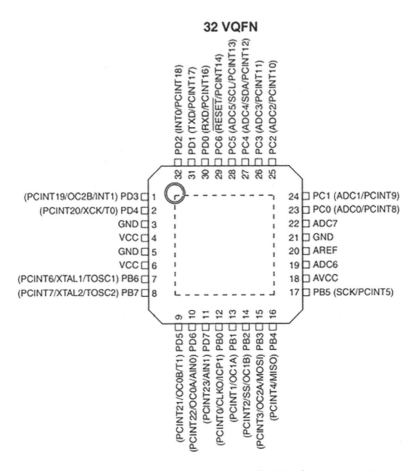

Figure 1-8. *Very thin Quad Flat No-lead (VQFN) version of ATmega328*

The connection between ATmega328 pins and Arduino UNO board pins is shown in Figure 1-9. For example, ATmega328's PC2 and PD5 pins are connected to pins A2 and 5 of the Arduino UNO board.

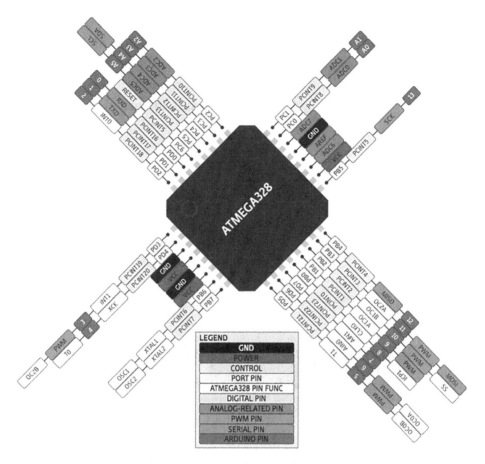

Figure 1-9. *Connection between ATmega328 microcontroller pins and Arduino UNO pins*

1.6 Programming the Arduino Boards

Arduino boards can be programmed in different ways. In this book, we will use the C programming in order to program the Arduino board. Arduino boards can be programmed using visual environments and other languages (e.g., Python) as well.

We will write the C code in the Arduino Integrated Development Environment (IDE). The Arduino IDE (Figure 1-10) contains a text editor for writing code, a message area, a text console, a toolbar with buttons for common functions, and a series of menus. It connects to the Arduino hardware to upload programs and communicate with them.

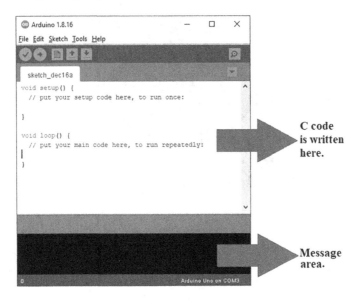

Figure 1-10. *Arduino IDE*

Programs written using the Arduino IDE are called sketches. These sketches are written in the text editor and are saved with the file .ino extension.

As shown in Figure 1-10, the C code has two default functions: setup and loop. The code inside the void setup will be executed once, and only once, at the beginning of the program. Then, the code inside the void loop will be executed again and again (hence the name "loop"), until you power off the Arduino board.

1.7 Downloading the Arduino IDE

You can download the Arduino IDE using the `www.arduino.cc/en/` `software` link. Use the DOWNLOAD OPTIONS section (Figure 1-11) of the given link to download the suitable version for your computer.

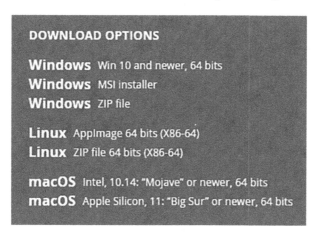

Figure 1-11. *Download section of the Arduino website*

1.8 HEX File

A HEX file is a hexadecimal source file typically used in the programming of microcontrollers. If you share a .INO file, anyone can edit or see the main program. But HEX files are much more secure than INO files; no one can edit them because of the hexadecimal format.

Let's see how we can see the generated HEX file associated with a C code. Open the Arduino IDE (Figure 1-12).

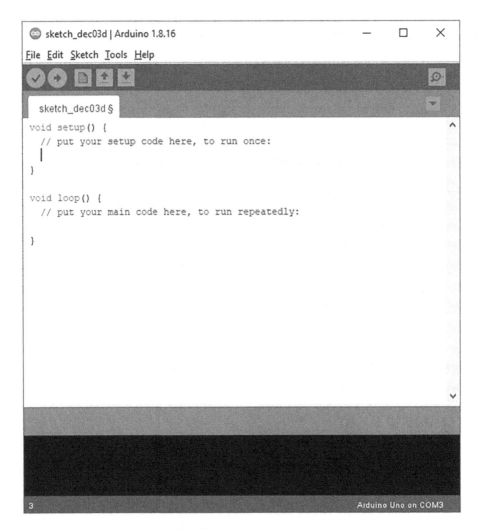

Figure 1-12. *An empty sketch*

Write the code shown in Figure 1-13. This code turns on the onboard LED, waits for 1 s, turns off the onboard LED, waits for 1 s, and repeats this procedure.

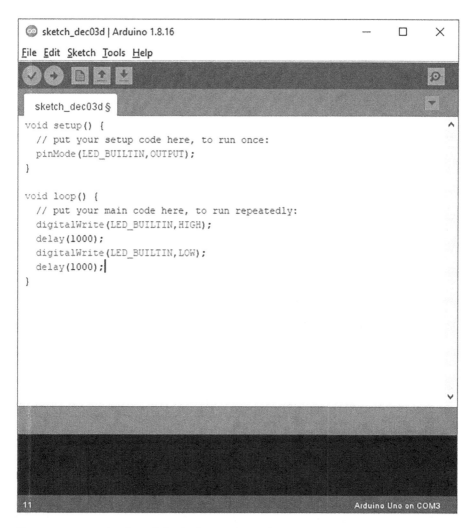

Figure 1-13. Code to blink the onboard LED

Click File ➤ Save or press Ctrl+S. This opens the Save sketch folder as... window for you (Figure 1-14). Save the file with the name of blink.

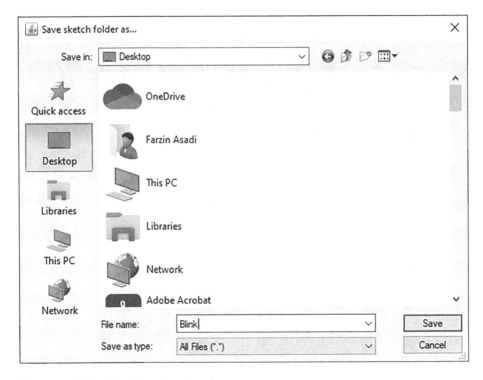

Figure 1-14. *Saving the sketch*

Click File ➤ Preferences (Figure 1-15).

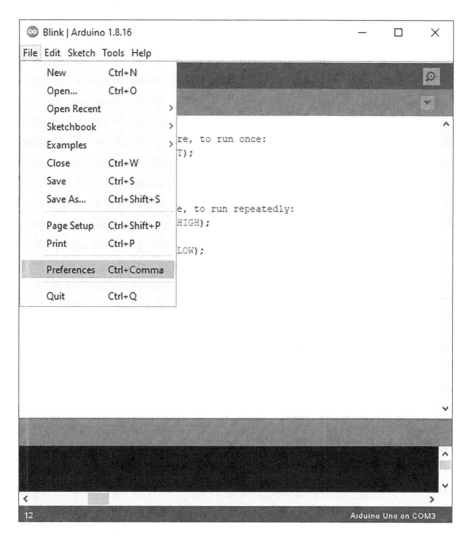

Figure 1-15. *File ➤ Preferences*

Check the compilation box (Figure 1-16).

17

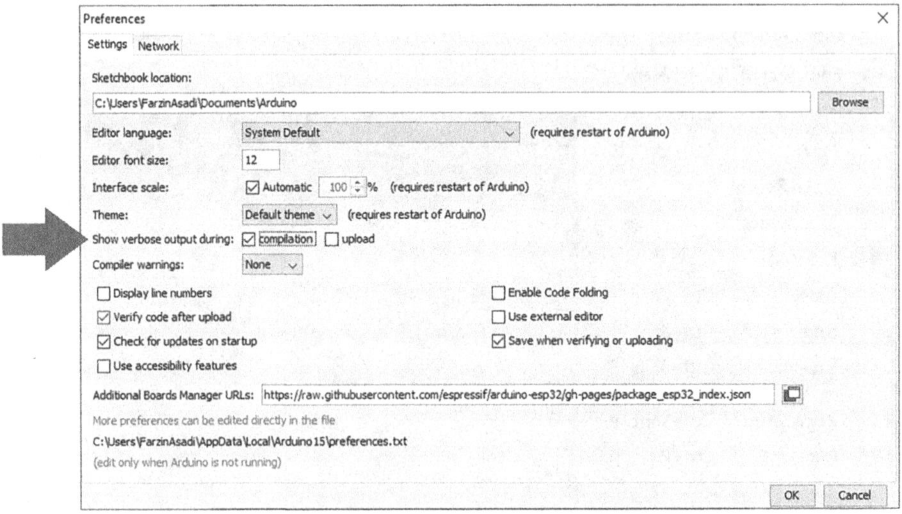

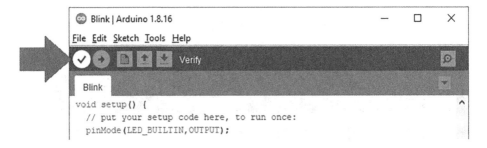

Figure 1-16. *Preferences window*

Click the Verify button (Figure 1-17). Wait until "Done compiling" appears on the screen (Figure 1-18).

Figure 1-17. *Verify button*

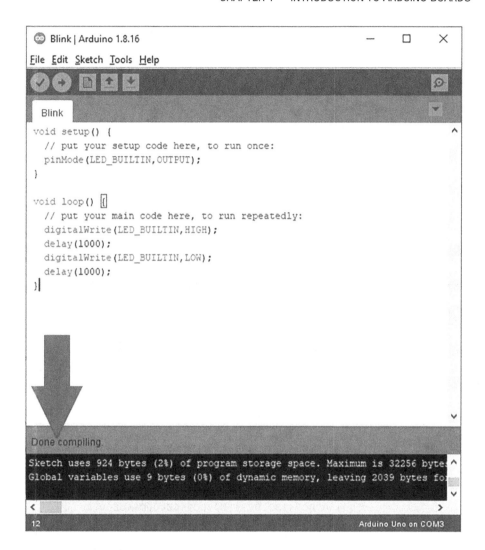

Figure 1-18. *Compiling is done*

Now go to C:\Users\Your_Name\AppData\Local\Temp\. The generated HEX file is located there (Figure 1-19).

Name	Date modified	Type	Size
core	03.12.2022 06:25	File folder	
libraries	03.12.2022 06:25	File folder	
preproc	03.12.2022 06:25	File folder	
sketch	03.12.2022 06:28	File folder	
Blink.ino.eep	03.12.2022 06:28	EEP File	1 KB
Blink.ino.elf	03.12.2022 06:28	ELF File	14 KB
Blink.ino.hex	03.12.2022 06:28	HEX File	3 KB
Blink.ino.with_bootloader.bin	03.12.2022 06:28	BIN File	32 KB
Blink.ino.with_bootloader.hex	03.12.2022 06:28	HEX File	4 KB
build.options	03.12.2022 06:28	JSON File	2 KB
includes.cache	03.12.2022 06:28	CACHE File	1 KB

Figure 1-19. *Generated HEX file*

You can use Notepad++ to open the HEX file (Figure 1-20). As the name suggests, it contains a collection of HEX numbers.

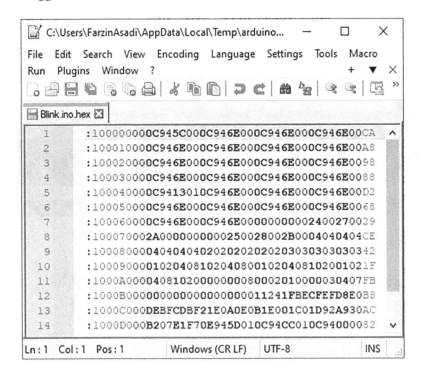

Figure 1-20. *Notepad++ is used to open the generated HEX file*

1.9 Uploading a Program onto the Arduino Board

Connect the Arduino UNO to the computer using its cable. Open the Tools and select the Board: "Arduino UNO" (Figure 1-21).

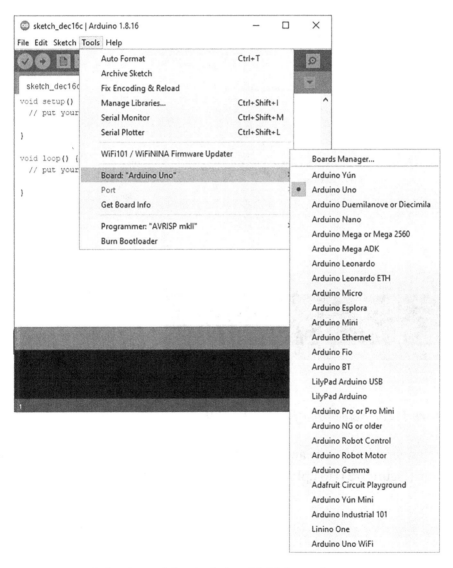

Figure 1-21. *Selection of the Arduino UNO board*

AVRISP mkII is good for Arduino UNO. Ensure that it is selected (Figure 1-22).

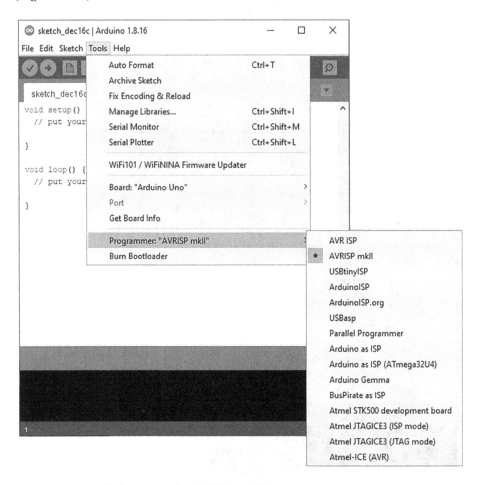

Figure 1-22. *Selection of AVRISP mkII*

Now write your code and save it (Figure 1-23). Then click the Upload button (Figure 1-24) to upload the code into the Arduino board.

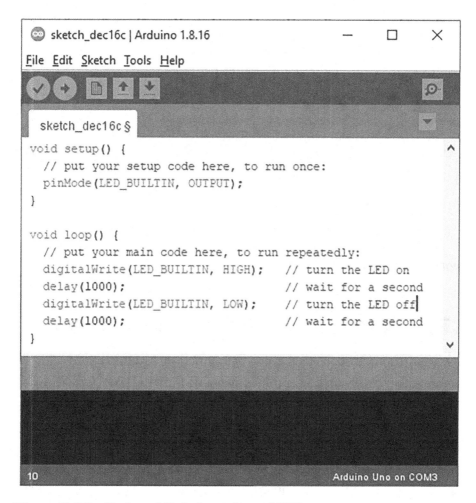

Figure 1-23. *Code to blink the onboard LED*

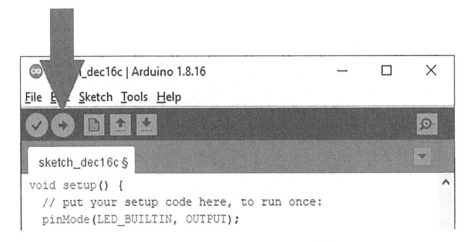

Figure 1-24. *Upload button*

1.10 Power Supply for the Arduino Board

All Arduino boards need electric power to function. Arduino boards can operate satisfactorily on power that is available from the USB port. The USB port is used as the source of energy in all of the examples in this book.

Another way to power your board is by supplying voltage from a regulated DC power source directly to the VIN pin (Figure 1-25). Just need to connect the positive wire from your power supply to VIN and the negative to GND. Follow your board power specifications to figure out the voltage range that your board can handle. For the Arduino UNO board, 7 V<VIN<12 V is suitable. Note that the VIN pin is an INPUT only.

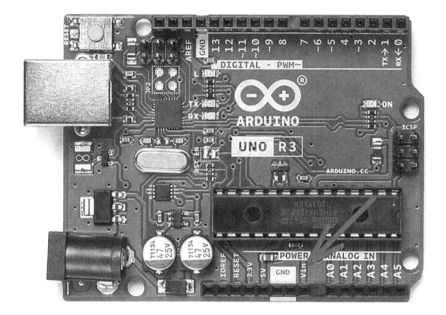

Figure 1-25. *Vin pin of Arduino*

Some Arduino boards like UNO, MEGA, and DUE come with a DC socket that can be used to power the boards (Figure 1-26). In this method, a power supply adapter that provides 7–12 V DC is required.

5.5mm/2.1mm DC Barrel Plug
Centre Positive
Recommended 6V – 12VDC

Figure 1-26. *Barrel jack to supply the Arduino from an external power source*

1.11 Ready-to-Use Examples

You can find ready-to-use examples in the File ➤ Examples section (Figure 1-27). Note that each example may need a specific hardware configuration. Hardware details are written as comment in the first lines of the code.

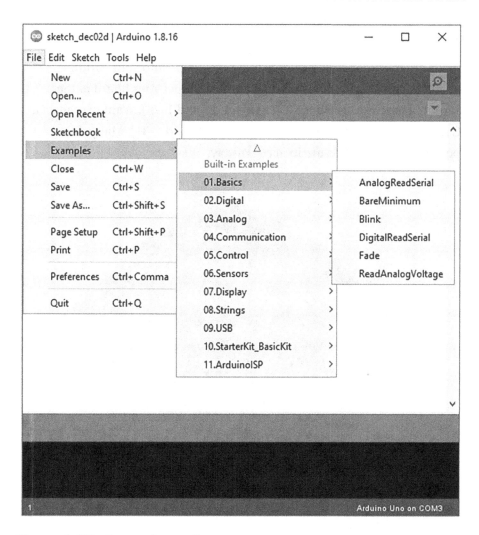

Figure 1-27. *Examples section*

1.12 Arduino Shields

Shields are modular circuit boards that piggyback onto your Arduino
to instill it with extra functionality. Want to connect your board to the
Internet? There is a shield for it (Figures 1-28 and 1-29). Want to control a
DC motor? There is a shield for it (Figures 1-30 and 1-31). Many different
types of Arduino shields are in access today.

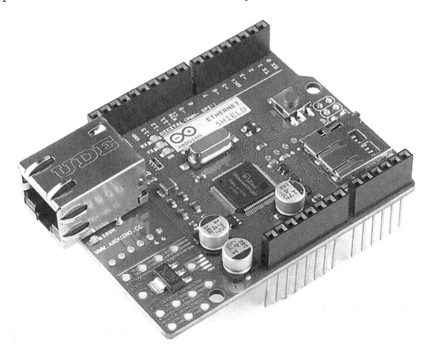

Figure 1-28. *Ethernet shield*

Figure 1-29. *An Ethernet shield is connected to the Arduino board*

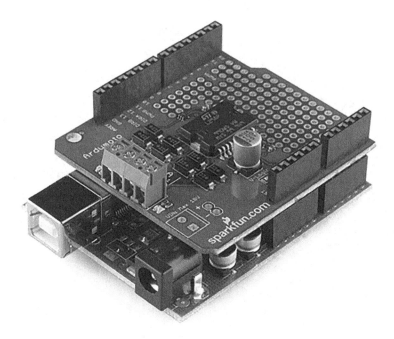

Figure 1-30. *A motor shield is connected to the Arduino board*

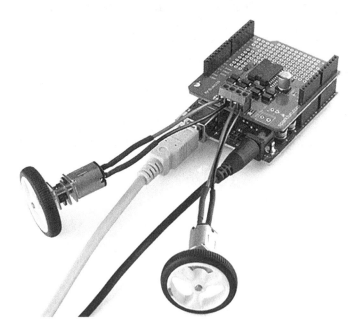

Figure 1-31. *Two motors are controlled with a motor shield*

1.13 Language Reference

The Language Reference section of the Arduino website (`www.arduino.cc/reference/en/`) is the best reference to learn the C programming of Arduino boards. Don't forget to visit there.

1.14 References for Further Study

[1] List of Arduino boards:
`https://bit.ly/2FmLorr`

[2] Schematic of Arduino UNO revision 3:
`https://bit.ly/3ju9NRw`

[3] ATmega328 datasheet:
`https://bit.ly/3I5ej30`

[4] Different ways to power an Arduino board:
`https://bit.ly/3YTKet5`

CHAPTER 2

Digital Input/Output (I/O)

2.1 Introduction

A digital signal is a signal that represents data as a sequence of discrete values; at any given time, it can only take on, at most, one of a finite number of values. This contrasts with an analog signal, which represents continuous values; at any given time, it represents a real number within a continuous range of values.

In this chapter, you will learn how to use the Arduino board to read or generate digital signals. According to Figure 2-1, pins 0–13 are digital pins, and they can be used as digital input or output (I/O). Pins which have a tilde (~) symbol behind them (pins 3, 5, 6, 9, 10, and 11) can be used for pulse width modulation (PWM) purposes as well. PWM is studied in Chapter 7. Pins 0 and 1 are used to transmit and receive the serial data as well. Therefore, it is a good idea not to use them as digital I/O when your project contains serial communication.

© Farzin Asadi 2023
F. Asadi, *Essentials of Arduino™ Boards Programming*, Maker Innovations Series,
https://doi.org/10.1007/978-1-4842-9600-4_2

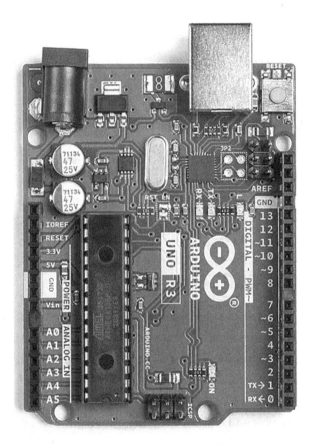

Figure 2-1. *Arduino UNO board*

Digital pins can be configured as either inputs or outputs. Simply, an input signal with a value of less than 2.2 V is considered low, and an input signal with a value bigger than 2.6 V is considered high. Figure 2-2 shows the input-output relation in a more accurate manner. As shown in Figure 2-2, a hysteresis loop exists in the graph.

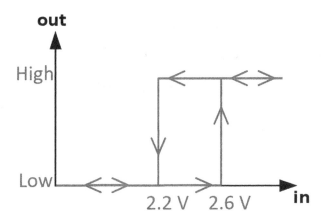

Figure 2-2. *Input-output characteristic for an input pin*

2.2 Properties of Pins Configured As Input

Arduino pins default to inputs, so they don't need to be explicitly declared as inputs with the pinMode command when they are used as inputs (however, explicitly declaring the pin with the pinMode command is recommended).

Pins configured this way are said to be in a high-impedance state. Input pins make extremely small demands on the circuit that they are sampling, equivalent to a series resistor of 100 MΩ in front of the pin. This means that it takes very little current to move the input pin from one state to another, and can make the pins useful for such tasks as implementing a capacitive touch sensor, reading an LED as a photodiode, or reading an analog sensor with a scheme such as RCTime. This also means, however, that pins configured with the pinMode command with nothing connected to them, or with wires connected to them that are not connected to other circuits, will report seemingly random changes in pin state, picking up electrical noise from the environment or capacitively coupling the state of a nearby pin.

2.3 Pull-Up or Pull-Down Resistors with Pins Configured As Input

Often, it is useful to steer an input pin to a known state if no input is present. This can be done by adding a pull-up resistor (to +5 V) or a pull-down resistor (to ground) on the input (Figures 2-3 and 2-4). A 10 kΩ resistor is a good value for a pull-up or pull-down resistor.

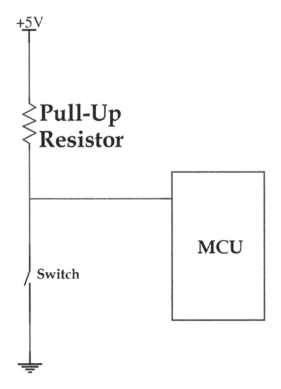

Figure 2-3. *Pull-up resistor*

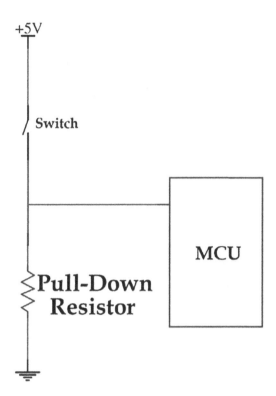

Figure 2-4. *Pull-down resistor*

2.4 Properties of Pins Configured As INPUT_PULLUP

There are pull-up resistors built into the ATmega chip that can be accessed from software. Such internal resistors can eliminate the need for external pull-up resistors. The value of this pull-up resistor depends on the microcontroller used. On most AVR-based boards, the value is guaranteed to be between 20 kΩ and 50 kΩ.

When connecting a sensor to a pin configured with INPUT_PULLUP, the other end should be connected to the ground (Figure 2-5). In the case of a simple switch, this causes the pin to read HIGH when the switch is open and LOW when the switch is pressed.

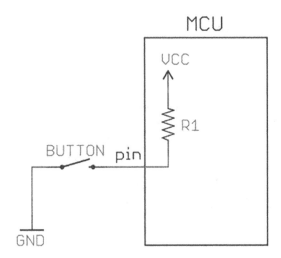

Figure 2-5. *Internal pull-up resistor*

2.5 Properties of Pins Configured As OUTPUT

Pins configured as output with the pinMode() command are said to be in a low-impedance state. This means that they can provide a substantial amount of current to other circuits connected to the microcontroller.

ATmega pins can source (give) up to 40 mA of current to other devices/circuits. This is enough current to brightly light up an LED (don't forget the series Rs resistor shown in Figure 2-6) or run many sensors, for example, but not enough current to run most relays, solenoids, or motors. High and low levels are associated with +5 V and 0 V, respectively.

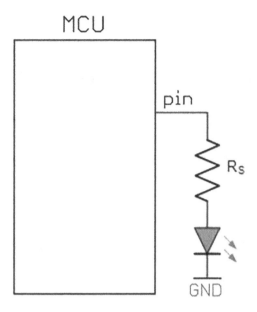

Figure 2-6. *Connecting an LED to a microcontroller pin* *(220 Ω<Rs<470 Ω)*

Short circuits on Arduino pins, or attempting to run high current devices from them, can damage or destroy the output transistors in the pin or damage the entire ATmega chip. Often, this will result in a "dead" pin in the microcontroller, but the remaining chip will still function adequately. For this reason, it is a good idea to connect output pins to other devices with 470 Ω or 1 kΩ resistors, unless maximum current draw from the pins is required for a particular application.

2.6 Blinking the Onboard LED

In this section, you will learn how to generate digital outputs. An LED shows the generated digital signal. When the generated signal is high, the LED is turned on. When the generated digital signal is low, the LED is off.

The Arduino boards have an onboard LED. So, there is no need to connect an external LED to the board in order to see the generated digital signal. In the Arduino UNO board, the onboard LED is connected to pin 13. Upload the following code to the Arduino board:

```
const int LED=LED_BUILTIN;
void setup() {
  // put your setup code here, to run once:
  pinMode(LED,OUTPUT);
}

void loop() {
  // put your main code here, to run repeatedly:
  digitalWrite(LED,HIGH);
  delay(1000);
  digitalWrite(LED,LOW);
  delay(1000);
}
```

After uploading the code to the Arduino board, you will see that the onboard LED starts to blink: it is on for one second, and it is off for one second. You can use any integer numbers instead of using HIGH and LOW constants. Any nonzero integer generates a high signal (i.e., +5 V), and zero generates a low signal (i.e., 0 V). For instance, the previous code can be written as follows as well:

```
const int LED=LED_BUILTIN;
void setup() {
  // put your setup code here, to run once:
  pinMode(LED,OUTPUT);
}
```

```
void loop() {
  // put your main code here, to run repeatedly:
  digitalWrite(LED,1);
  delay(1000);
  digitalWrite(LED,0);
  delay(1000);
}
```

You can use Boolean variables as well:

```
const int LED=LED_BUILTIN;
void setup() {
  // put your setup code here, to run once:
  pinMode(LED,OUTPUT);
}

void loop() {
  // put your main code here, to run repeatedly:
  digitalWrite(LED,true);
  delay(1000);
  digitalWrite(LED,false);
  delay(1000);
}
```

2.7 Delay Generation with the millis Function

The millis function returns the number of milliseconds passed since the Arduino board began running the current program. This number will overflow (go back to zero) after approximately 50 days. In the previous example, we used the delay function to generate the required delay. In this example, we will use the millis function to generate the required one-second delay:

```
unsigned long t0=0;
unsigned long t1=0;

void setup() {
  // put your setup code here, to run once:
  pinMode(LED_BUILTIN, OUTPUT);
}

void loop() {
  // put your main code here, to run repeatedly:
  t0=millis();
  digitalWrite(LED_BUILTIN, HIGH);
  while (millis()<(t0+1000)){
  }

  t1=millis();
  digitalWrite(LED_BUILTIN, LOW);
  while (millis()<(t1+1000)){
  }
}
```

After uploading the preceding code to the Arduino board, you will see that the onboard LED starts to blink.

2.8 Measurement of Time Used to Run the Commands

In this example, we will use the micros command to measure the time required to run the digitalWrite command. In this example, we will use the micros function. This function returns the number of microseconds since the Arduino board began running the current program. This number will overflow (go back to zero) after approximately 70 minutes. On 16 MHz Arduino boards (e.g., UNO, DUE, and Nano), this function has a resolution of four microseconds (i.e., the value returned is always a multiple of four). Upload the following code to the Arduino board:

```
const int LED=LED_BUILTIN;
double t0=0;
double t1=0;
double t2=0;

void setup() {
  // put your setup code here, to run once:
  pinMode(LED,OUTPUT);
  Serial.begin(9600);
}

void loop() {
  // put your main code here, to run repeatedly:
    t0=micros();
    digitalWrite(LED,HIGH);
    t1=micros();
    digitalWrite(LED,LOW);
    t2=micros();
    Serial.println((String)"digitalWrite(LED,HIGH) requires:
    "+(t1-t0)+" us.");
```

```
Serial.println((String)"digitalWrite(LED,LOW) requires:
"+(t2-t1)+" us.");
Serial.println();
delay(1000);
}
```

The code of this example used serial communication to show the measured values. Serial communication is studied in Chapter 5. After uploading the code to the board, click Tools ➤ Serial Monitor (Figure 2-7) in order to see the result (Figure 2-8).

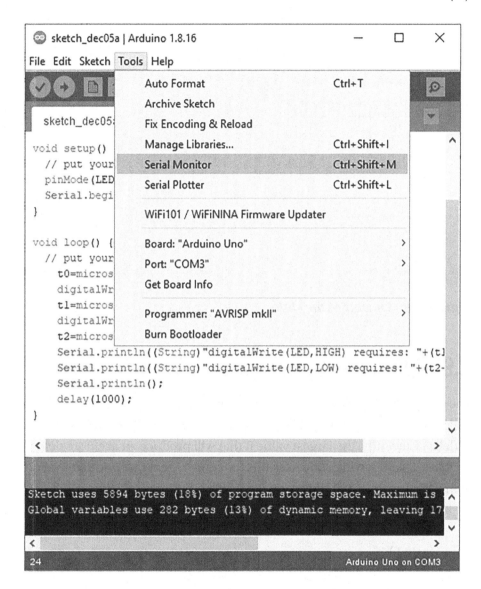

Figure 2-7. *Tools ➤ Serial Monitor*

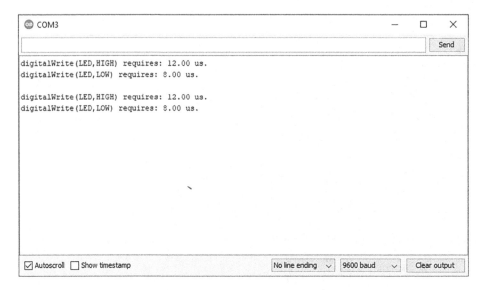

Figure 2-8. *Output of the code*

2.9 Delay in the Range of Microseconds

The delay command generates delay in the range of milliseconds. The delayMicroseconds(n) command can be used to generate n microseconds of delay. Currently, the largest value n that will produce an accurate delay is 16383. The following code uses this function to generate a square wave with a frequency of 500 Hz:

```
int pin = 2;

void setup() {
    pinMode(pin, OUTPUT); // sets the digital pin as output
}
```

```
void loop() {
    digitalWrite(pin, HIGH);
    delayMicroseconds(1000);
    digitalWrite(pin, LOW);
    delayMicroseconds(1000);
}
```

After uploading the code to the board, connect an oscilloscope to pin 2 in order to ensure that the frequency of generated square waveform is 50 Hz.

2.10 Blink Two LEDs

In this example, we want to blink two LEDs with two different time delays. The first LED is on for 500 ms and is off for 500 ms. The second LED is on for 400 ms and is off for 400 ms. The waveform that needs to be applied to the LEDs is shown in Figure 2-9.

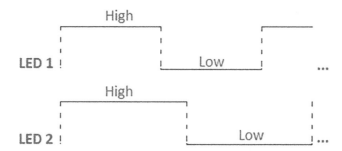

Figure 2-9. *Pattern of voltage for LED 1 and LED 2*

Upload the following code to the Arduino board. In this code, the output voltage is determined by two arrays. Each number in the arrays determines the corresponding output for a 100 ms interval. For instance, the third value of LED1Array is 1. This means that LED 1 is high for the [200 ms, 300 ms] interval.

```
//obtaining two different delays
//LED1 delay is 400 ms (400 ms on 400 ms off)
//LED2 delay is 500 ms (500 ms on 500 ms off)
//This example uses the array

const int LED1=8;
const int LED2=9;
int LED1State=HIGH;
int LED2State=HIGH;
int k=0;

int LED1Array[]={1,1,1,1,0,0,0,0,1,1,1,1,0,0,0,0,1,1,1,1,0,0,0,
0,1,1,1,1,0,0,0,0,1,1,1,1,0,0,0,0};
int LED2Array[]={1,1,1,1,1,0,0,0,0,0,1,1,1,1,1,0,0,0,0,0,1,1,1,
1,1,0,0,0,0,0,1,1,1,1,1,0,0,0,0,0};

void setup() {
  // put your setup code here, to run once:
  pinMode(LED1,OUTPUT);
  pinMode(LED2,OUTPUT);
  digitalWrite(LED1,LED1State);
  digitalWrite(LED2,LED2State);
}

void loop() {
  // put your main code here, to run repeatedly:
  delay(100);
  k=k+1;
  digitalWrite(LED1,LED1Array[k-1]);
  digitalWrite(LED2,LED2Array[k-1]);
  if (k==40) k=0;
}
```

Connect two LEDs to pins 8 and 9 of Arduino (Figure 2-10). The LEDs start to blink with two different periods. Resistors R1 and R2 limit the current drawn from the port.

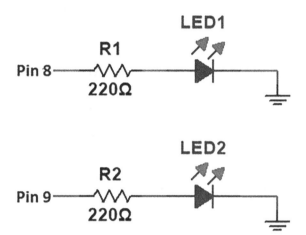

Figure 2-10. *Two LEDs are connected to pins 8 and 9*

The following points help you to determine the anode and cathode of an LED easily:

a) LEDs have one lead that is longer than the other. This longer lead is the anode, and the shorter one is the cathode. Note that we assumed that the leads have not been clipped (Figure 2-11).

b) There is a small flat notch on the side of the LED. The lead that is closer to the notch is always the cathode (Figure 2-11).

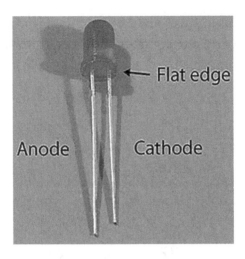

Figure 2-11. *Anode and cathode of an LED*

2.11 RGB LED

An RGB LED is a combination of red, green, and blue LEDs put into a single package. RGB LEDs can be used to produce almost any color by controlling the intensity of red, green, and blue lights that LEDs produce. RGB LEDs can be used in different applications such as outdoor decoration lighting, stage lighting designs, home decoration lighting, LED matrix display, and more.

RGB LEDs are divided into two groups: common cathode RGB LEDs (Figure 2-12) and common anode RGB LEDs (Figure 2-13).

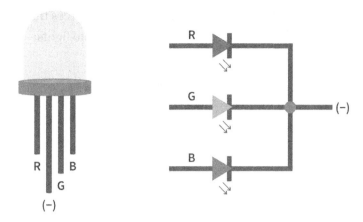

Figure 2-12. *Common cathode RGB LED*

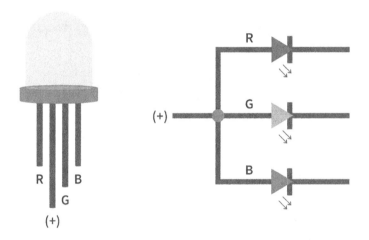

Figure 2-13. *Common anode RGB LED*

In this section, we will study the common cathode RGB LED. The cathodes of common cathode RGB LEDs are connected to ground. When you send the high signal to the anodes, the corresponding LED is turned on.

51

Upload the following code to the board. This code forces the common cathode RGB LED to produce red, green, blue, and white lights:

```
//Common Cathode RGB LED.
//Cathode is connected to GND pin of Arduino.

#define Rpin 8
#define Gpin 9
#define Bpin 10

void setup() {
  // put your setup code here, to run once:
  pinMode(Rpin, OUTPUT);
  pinMode(Gpin, OUTPUT);
  pinMode(Bpin, OUTPUT);
}

void loop() {
  // put your main code here, to run repeatedly:
  digitalWrite(Rpin,HIGH);
  delay(1000);
  digitalWrite(Rpin,LOW);
  digitalWrite(Gpin,HIGH);
  delay(1000);
  digitalWrite(Gpin,LOW);
  digitalWrite(Bpin,HIGH);
  delay(1000);
  digitalWrite(Bpin,LOW);
  digitalWrite(Rpin,HIGH);
  digitalWrite(Gpin,HIGH);
  digitalWrite(Bpin,HIGH);
  delay(1000);
  digitalWrite(Rpin,LOW);
```

```
  digitalWrite(Gpin,LOW);
  digitalWrite(Bpin,LOW);
}
```

Connect the common cathode RGB LED to pins 8, 9, and 10 (Figure 2-14). The RGB LED starts to produce different colors.

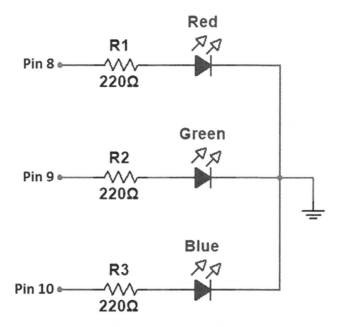

Figure 2-14. *Connecting the common cathode RGB LED to Arduino*

Let's write the code for common anode RGB LEDs as well. The anodes of common anode RGB LEDs are connected to +5 V. When you send the low signal to the cathodes, the corresponding LED is turned on.

Upload the following code to the board. This code forces the common anode RGB LED to produce red, green, blue, and white lights:

```
//Common Anode RGB LED.
//Anode is connected to +5 pin of Arduino.
```

```
#define Rpin 8
#define Gpin 9
#define Bpin 10

void setup() {
  // put your setup code here, to run once:
  pinMode(Rpin, OUTPUT);
  pinMode(Gpin, OUTPUT);
  pinMode(Bpin, OUTPUT);
}

void loop() {
  // put your main code here, to run repeatedly:
  digitalWrite(Rpin,LOW);
  delay(1000);
  digitalWrite(Rpin,HIGH);
  digitalWrite(Gpin,LOW);
  delay(1000);
  digitalWrite(Gpin,HIGH);
  digitalWrite(Bpin,LOW);
  delay(1000);
  digitalWrite(Bpin,HIGH);
  digitalWrite(Rpin,LOW);
  digitalWrite(Gpin,LOW);
  digitalWrite(Bpin,LOW);
  delay(1000);
  digitalWrite(Rpin,HIGH);
  digitalWrite(Gpin,HIGH);
  digitalWrite(Bpin,HIGH);
}
```

Connect the common anode RGB LED to pins 8, 9, and 10 (Figure 2-15). The RGB LED starts to produce different colors.

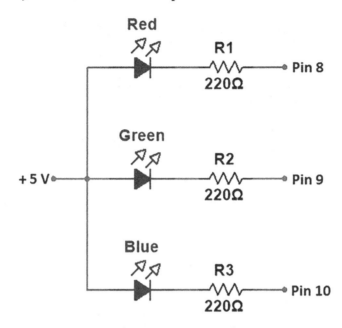

Figure 2-15. *Connecting the common anode RGB LED to Arduino*

2.12 One-Digit Decimal Counter

In this section, we want to use a seven-segment display (Figure 2-16) to make a one-digit (i.e., from 0 to 9) counter. A seven-segment display is nothing more than seven LEDs put into a single package. LEDs can be connected in common cathode (Figure 2-17) or common anode (Figure 2-18) configurations.

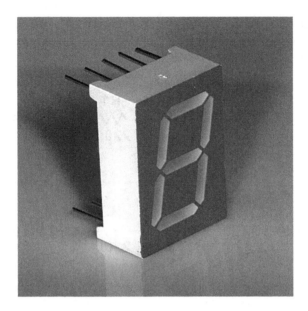

Figure 2-16. *Seven-segment display*

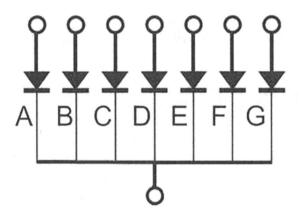

Figure 2-17. *Schematic of a common cathode seven-segment display*

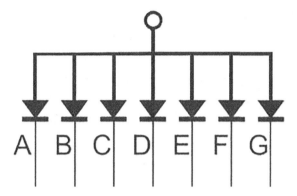

Figure 2-18. *Schematic of a common anode seven-segment display*

Sometimes, seven-segment displays have eight LEDs. The eighth LED is used to show the decimal point (DP). Figure 2-19 shows a seven-segment display with a decimal point. This display has eight LEDs.

Figure 2-19. *Seven-segment display with a decimal point*

Figure 2-20 shows how different values can be displayed on the seven-segment display. Table 2-1 summarizes this figure. In this figure, activated segments are shown with 1. For instance, in order to show number 3, segments a, b, c, d, and g must be turned on.

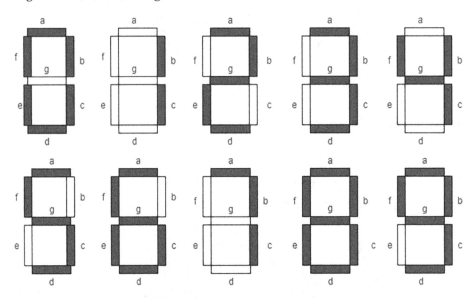

Figure 2-20. *Displaying different numbers with a seven-segment display*

Table 2-1. *Truth table for each decimal digit displayed on a seven-segment display*

Decimal Digit	Individual Segment Illuminated						
	a	b	c	d	e	f	g
0	1	1	1	1	1	1	0
1	0	1	1	0	0	0	0
2	1	1	0	1	1	0	1
3	1	1	1	1	0	0	1
4	0	1	1	0	0	1	1
5	1	0	1	1	0	1	1
6	1	0	1	1	1	1	1
7	1	1	1	0	0	0	0
8	1	1	1	1	1	1	1
9	1	1	1	1	0	1	1

Let's write a code to display numbers 0–9 on a common cathode display. Upload the following code to the board:

```
const int a=2;
const int b=3;
const int c=4;
const int d=5;
const int e=6;
const int f=7;
const int g=8;
int i=0;
void displayNumber(int n);
void clearDisp();
```

```
void setup() {
  pinMode(a,OUTPUT);
  pinMode(b,OUTPUT);
  pinMode(c,OUTPUT);
  pinMode(d,OUTPUT);
  pinMode(e,OUTPUT);
  pinMode(f,OUTPUT);
  pinMode(g,OUTPUT);
}

void loop() {
  // put your main code here, to run repeatedly:
  for (i=0;i<=9;i++){
    displayNumber(i);
    delay(1000);
  }
}

void clearDisp(){
  digitalWrite(a,LOW);
  digitalWrite(b,LOW);
  digitalWrite(c,LOW);
  digitalWrite(d,LOW);
  digitalWrite(e,LOW);
  digitalWrite(f,LOW);
  digitalWrite(g,LOW);
}

void displayNumber(int n)
{
switch (n){
  case 0:
  clearDisp();
```

```
digitalWrite(a,HIGH);
digitalWrite(b,HIGH);
digitalWrite(c,HIGH);
digitalWrite(d,HIGH);
digitalWrite(e,HIGH);
digitalWrite(f,HIGH);
digitalWrite(g,LOW);
  break;

case 1:
clearDisp();
digitalWrite(a,LOW);
digitalWrite(b,HIGH);
digitalWrite(c,HIGH);
digitalWrite(d,LOW);
digitalWrite(e,LOW);
digitalWrite(f,LOW);
digitalWrite(g,LOW);
  break;

case 2:
clearDisp();
digitalWrite(a,HIGH);
digitalWrite(b,HIGH);
digitalWrite(c,LOW);
digitalWrite(d,HIGH);
digitalWrite(e,HIGH);
digitalWrite(f,LOW);
digitalWrite(g,HIGH);
  break;
```

```
case 3:
clearDisp();
digitalWrite(a,HIGH);
digitalWrite(b,HIGH);
digitalWrite(c,HIGH);
digitalWrite(d,HIGH);
digitalWrite(e,LOW);
digitalWrite(f,LOW);
digitalWrite(g,HIGH);
  break;

case 4:
clearDisp();
digitalWrite(a,LOW);
digitalWrite(b,HIGH);
digitalWrite(c,HIGH);
digitalWrite(d,LOW);
digitalWrite(e,LOW);
digitalWrite(f,HIGH);
digitalWrite(g,HIGH);
  break;

case 5:
clearDisp();
digitalWrite(a,HIGH);
digitalWrite(b,LOW);
digitalWrite(c,HIGH);
digitalWrite(d,HIGH);
digitalWrite(e,LOW);
digitalWrite(f,HIGH);
digitalWrite(g,HIGH);
  break;
```

```
case 6:
clearDisp();
digitalWrite(a,HIGH);
digitalWrite(b,LOW);
digitalWrite(c,HIGH);
digitalWrite(d,HIGH);
digitalWrite(e,HIGH);
digitalWrite(f,HIGH);
digitalWrite(g,HIGH);
  break;

case 7:
clearDisp();
digitalWrite(a,HIGH);
digitalWrite(b,HIGH);
digitalWrite(c,HIGH);
digitalWrite(d,LOW);
digitalWrite(e,LOW);
digitalWrite(f,LOW);
digitalWrite(g,LOW);
  break;

case 8:
clearDisp();
digitalWrite(a,HIGH);
digitalWrite(b,HIGH);
digitalWrite(c,HIGH);
digitalWrite(d,HIGH);
digitalWrite(e,HIGH);
digitalWrite(f,HIGH);
digitalWrite(g,HIGH);
  break;
```

```
case 9:
clearDisp();
digitalWrite(a,HIGH);
digitalWrite(b,HIGH);
digitalWrite(c,HIGH);
digitalWrite(d,HIGH);
digitalWrite(e,LOW);
digitalWrite(f,HIGH);
digitalWrite(g,HIGH);
   break;
}
}
```

The hardware of this example is shown in Figure 2-21.

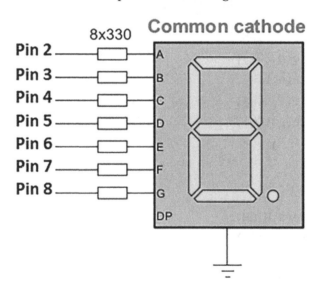

Figure 2-21. *Hardware of the studied example*

As an exercise, change the preceding code in order to show numbers on a common anode display.

2.13 Binary Counter

In this example, we want to make an 8-bit binary counter. We will use the Data Direction Register and Port Data Register for this purpose.

The Arduino UNO board uses the ATmega328 microcontroller. Figure 2-22 shows the connection between ATmega328 microcontroller pins and Arduino board pins. For instance, according to Figure 2-22, PB5 (6th bit of I/O port B) and PD2 (3rd bit of I/O port D) are connected to pins 13 and 2 of the Arduino UNO board, respectively.

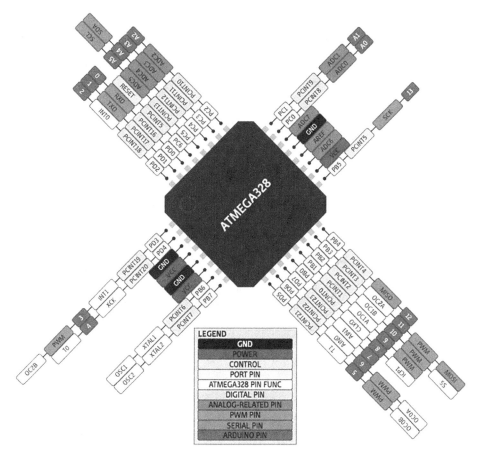

Figure 2-22. *Connection between ATmega328 microcontroller pins and Arduino UNO pins*

Tables 2-2 to 2-4 show the connection between ATmega328 I/O pins and Arduino UNO pins.

Table 2-2. *Port B's pins*

Port Bits	Arduino Pin
PB0	8
PB1	9
PB2	10
PB3	11
PB4	12
PB5	13

Table 2-3. *Port C's pins*

Port Bits	Arduino Pin
PC0	A0
PC1	A1
PC2	A2
PC3	A3
PC4	A4
PC5	A5

Table 2-4. *Port D's pins*

Port Bits	Arduino Pin
PD0	0
PD1	1
PD2	2
PD3	3
PD4	4
PD5	5
PD6	6
PD7	7

Upload the following code to your board. DDRD=0b11111111 makes ll of the port D pins output. A command like DDRD=0b11011100 defines the D0, D1, and D5 pins (pins 0, 1, and 5 of Arduino UNO) as input and the rest as output. The value that needs to be shown on port D is determined by the PORTD register.

```
// PORT
//See: https://create.arduino.cc/projecthub/Hack-star-Arduino/
learn-arduino-port-manipulation-2022-10f9af
//See: https://www.instructables.com/Arduino-and-Port-
Manipulation/
void setup() {
  // put your setup code here, to run once:
    DDRD=0b11111111;
}
```

```
void loop() {
  // put your main code here, to run repeatedly:
  for (int i=0;i<=255;i++){
   PORTD=i;
   delay(250);
  }
}
```

The hardware of this example is shown in Figure 2-23. The LED connected to pin 0 is the least significant bit (LSB), and the LED connected to pin 7 is the most significant bit (MSB).

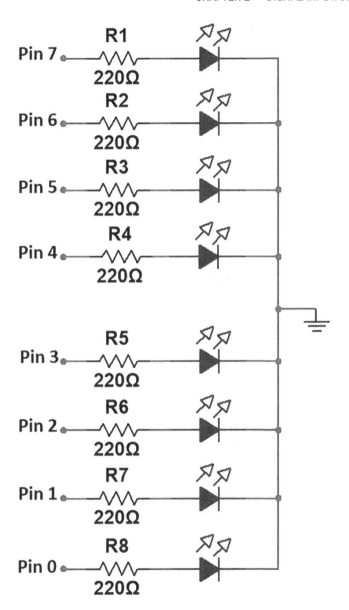

Figure 2-23. *Hardware of the studied example*

As an exercise, change the given program to work with the hardware shown in Figure 2-24. Note that you need a low signal (i.e., 0 V) in order to turn on the LEDs in Figure 2-24.

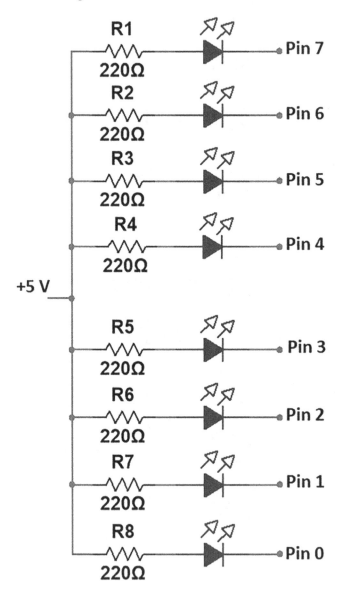

Figure 2-24. LEDs are connected in common anode configuration

2.14 Binary Counter with 74LS595 Shift Register

In the previous example, we used eight pins of Arduino in order to transfer the required data to the LEDs. You can use a 74LS595 shift register in order to decrease the number of microcontroller I/O ports used. The 74LS595 pinout is shown in Figure 2-25.

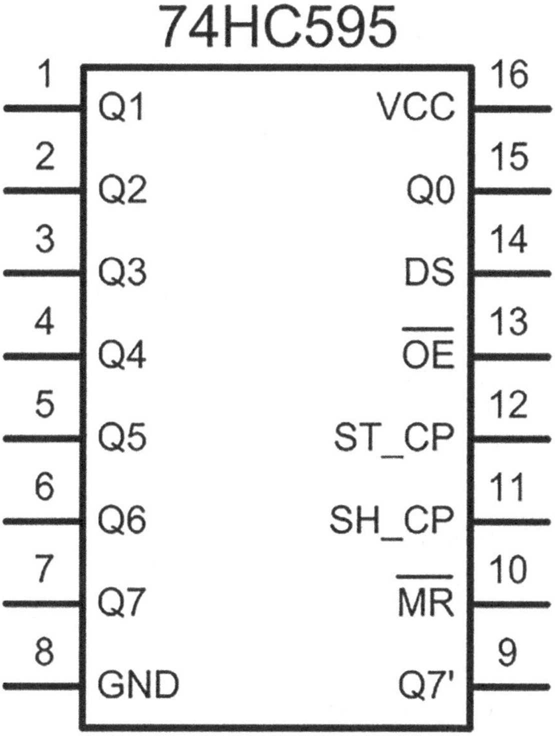

74HC595

1	Q1	VCC	16
2	Q2	Q0	15
3	Q3	DS	14
4	Q4	$\overline{OE}$	13
5	Q5	ST_CP	12
6	Q6	SH_CP	11
7	Q7	$\overline{MR}$	10
8	GND	Q7'	9

Figure 2-25. Pinout of 74HC595

Here, we want to make an 8-bit binary counter, but this time we will use only three I/O pins of the Arduino board. Upload the following code:

```
//Pin connected to 12 of 74HC595
int latchPin = 8;
```

```
//Pin connected to 11 of 74HC595
int clockPin = 12;
//Pin connected to 14 of 74HC595
int dataPin = 11;

void setup() {
// put your main code here, to run repeatedly:
pinMode(latchPin, OUTPUT);
pinMode(clockPin, OUTPUT);
pinMode(dataPin, OUTPUT);
}

void loop() {
// count from 0 to 255 and display the number
// on the LEDs
// bit:      7 6 5 4 3 2 1 0  (7 shows the MSB, 0 shows the LSB)
// IC pin:   7 6 5 4 3 2 1 15
for (int numberToDisplay = 0; numberToDisplay < 256;
numberToDisplay++) {
  // take the latchPin low so
  // the LEDs don't change while you're sending in bits:
  digitalWrite(latchPin, LOW);
  // shift out the bits:
  shiftOut(dataPin, clockPin, MSBFIRST, numberToDisplay);
  //take the latch pin high so the LEDs will light up:
  digitalWrite(latchPin, HIGH);
  // pause before next value:
  delay(500);
}
}
```

Connect pins 11, 12, and 14 of 74LS595 to pins 12, 8, and 11 of the Arduino board, respectively. Don't forget to connect the GND and +5 V of the Arduino board to pins 8 and 16 of 74LS595. LEDs are connected to the 74LS595 pins as shown in Figure 2-26 (IC-n shows pin n of 74LS595). The LED connected to pin 7 of the 74LS595 is the MSB, and the LED connected to pin 15 of 74LS595 is the LSB.

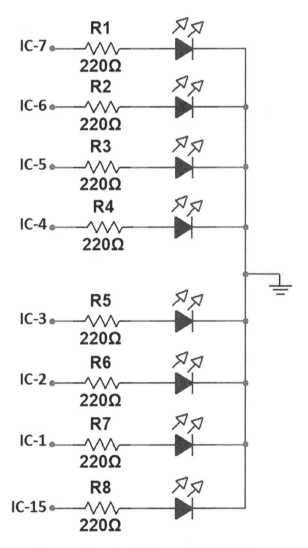

Figure 2-26. *Connecting the LEDs to 74HC595*

If you change the code to what is shown as follows (no change is applied to the hardware; only the shiftOut(dataPin, clockPin, MSBFIRST, numberToDisplay) command is changed to shiftOut(dataPin, clockPin, LSBFIRST, numberToDisplay)), then the LED connected to pin 7 of the IC shows the LSB, and the LED connected to pin 15 of the IC shows the MSB:

```
//Pin connected to 12 of 74HC595
int latchPin = 8;
//Pin connected to 11 of 74HC595
int clockPin = 12;
//Pin connected to 14 of 74HC595
int dataPin = 11;

void setup() {
// put your main code here, to run repeatedly:
pinMode(latchPin, OUTPUT);
pinMode(clockPin, OUTPUT);
pinMode(dataPin, OUTPUT);
}

void loop() {
// count from 0 to 255 and display the number
// on the LEDs
// bit:     7 6 5 4 3 2 1 0    (7 shows the MSB, 0 shows
                                the LSB)
// IC pin:  15 1 2 3 4 5 6 7
for (int numberToDisplay = 0; numberToDisplay < 256;
numberToDisplay++) {
  // take the latchPin low so
  // the LEDs don't change while you're sending in bits:
  digitalWrite(latchPin, LOW);
  // shift out the bits:
```

```
   shiftOut(dataPin, clockPin, LSBFIRST, numberToDisplay);
   //take the latch pin high so the LEDs will light up:
   digitalWrite(latchPin, HIGH);
   // pause before next value:
   delay(500);
   }
}
```

2.15 Four-Digit Display

74LS595 can be used to drive a four-digit display as well. This example shows how to drive a four-digit common anode display (Figure 2-27) with two 74LS595 ICs. Table 2-5 shows which code must be used for each digit. DP in this table represents the decimal point LED.

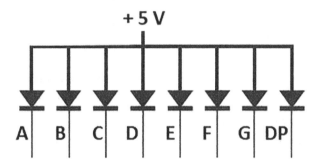

Figure 2-27. *Common anode display*

Table 2-5. *Truth table for each decimal digit displayed on a common anode seven segment*

Decimal Digit	Individual Segment Illuminated								HEX
	DP	G	f	e	d	c	b	a	
0	1	1	0	0	0	0	0	0	C0
1	1	1	1	1	1	0	0	1	F9
2	1	0	1	0	0	1	0	0	A4
3	1	0	1	1	0	0	0	0	B0
4	1	0	0	1	1	0	0	1	99
5	1	0	0	1	0	0	1	0	92
6	1	0	0	0	0	0	1	0	82
7	1	1	1	1	1	0	0	0	F8
8	1	0	0	0	0	0	0	0	80
9	1	0	0	1	0	0	0	0	90

For example, in order to show 1 on the display, we need to light segments b and c (Figure 2-28). The anode of all the LEDs inside the package is connected to VCC (Figure 2-27). Therefore, we need to send 0 to the cathode of segments b and c in order to light them (Figure 2-29).

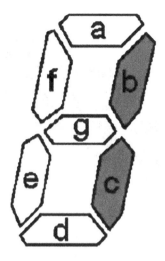

Figure 2-28. *Displaying 1 on the seven-segment display*

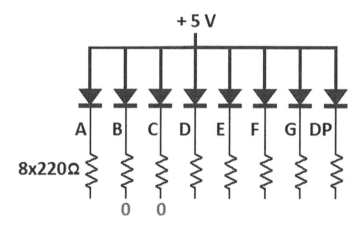

Figure 2-29. *Low must be given to B and C segments to display 1*

Figure 2-30 shows a four-digit common anode seven-segment display. The schematic of this display is shown in Figure 2-31.

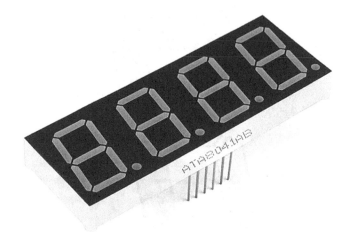

Figure 2-30. *Four-digit common anode display*

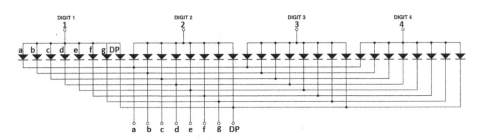

Figure 2-31. *Schematic of a four-digit common anode display*

Upload the following code to the Arduino board. This code shows 7890 on the display:

```
//This code is written for common Anode display.
#define LATCH_DIO 4
#define CLK_DIO 7
#define DATA_DIO 8

int digit1=0;
int digit2=0;
int digit3=0;
```

```
int digit4=0;

const byte SEGMENT_MAP[] ={0xC0,0xF9,0xA4,0xB0,0x99,0x92,
0x82,0xF8,0X80,0X90};
const byte SEGMENT_SELECT[] = {0xF1,0xF2,0xF4,0xF8};

void setup(){
  // put your setup code here, to run once:
  pinMode(LATCH_DIO,OUTPUT);
  pinMode(CLK_DIO,OUTPUT);
  pinMode(DATA_DIO,OUTPUT);
}

void loop(){
  // put your main code here, to run repeatedly:
  displayNumber(7890);
}

void displayNumber(int num){
  digit4 = num % 10;
  digit3 = (num / 10) % 10;
  digit2 = (num / 100) % 10;
  digit1 = (num / 1000) % 10;

  WriteNumberToSegment(0,digit1);
  WriteNumberToSegment(1,digit2);
  WriteNumberToSegment(2,digit3);
  WriteNumberToSegment(3,digit4);
}

void WriteNumberToSegment(byte Segment, byte Value){
digitalWrite(LATCH_DIO,LOW);
shiftOut(DATA_DIO, CLK_DIO, MSBFIRST, SEGMENT_MAP[Value]);
```

```
shiftOut(DATA_DIO, CLK_DIO, MSBFIRST, SEGMENT_
SELECT[Segment] );
digitalWrite(LATCH_DIO,HIGH);
}
```

The hardware of this example is shown in Figure 2-32. You can put 100 Ω resistors between IC and pins a, b, c, d, e, f, g, and DP of the display if you prefer lower light intensity.

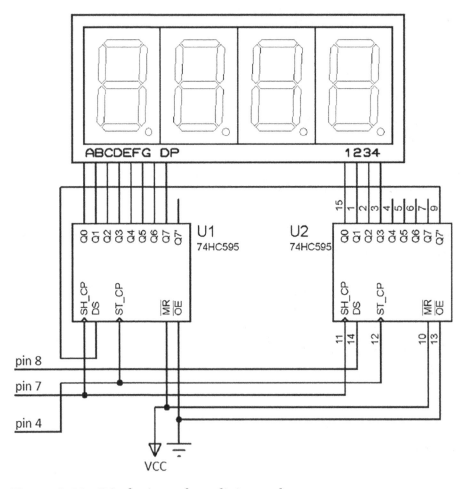

Figure 2-32. *Displaying a four-digit number on a common anode display*

2.16 TM1637 Four-Digit Display

The TM1637 (also called the Grove 4-Digit Display by Seeed Studio) is a seven-segment four-digit display that can be easily controlled with a few wires on Arduino (Figure 2-33).

This module is suitable for digital clock projects; however, it can be used in other projects which require to show a number between 0000 and 9999.

Figure 2-33. *TM1637 four-digit display*

Click Sketch ➤ Include Library ➤ Manage Libraries... (Figure 2-34). This opens the Library Manager window for you. Search for "tm1637" in this window (Figure 2-35) and install the library labeled "Grove 4-Digit Display" by Seeed Studio.

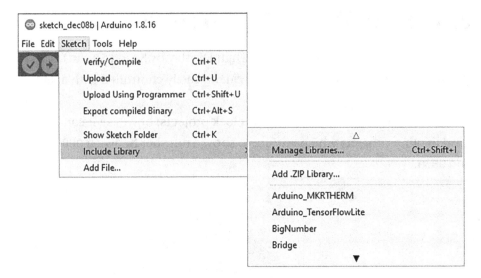

Figure 2-34. *Sketch* ➤ *Include Library* ➤ *Manage Libraries*

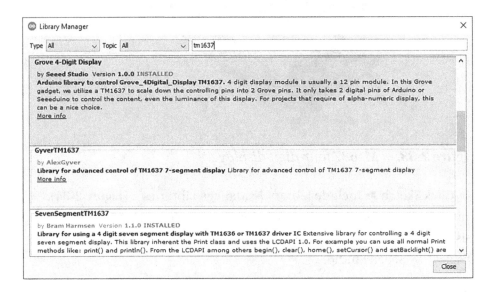

Figure 2-35. *Library Manager window*

The onboard four-digit LED on the TM1637 board has a four-digit seven-segment display. The seven-segment displays are labeled 0, 1, 2, and 3 as shown in Figure 2-36. The leftmost seven-segment display is 0.

Figure 2-36. *Label of seven segments*

The following code shows how to display 12:34 on the four-digit seven-segment display. Connect the CLK and DIO pins of the TM1637 board to pins 2 and 3 of the Arduino board, respectively. Don't forget to connect the VCC and GND pins of TM1637 to +5 and GND of Arduino.

```
#include <TM1637.h>
int CLK=2;
int DIO=3;
TM1637 tm(CLK,DIO);

void setup() {
  // put your setup code here, to run once:
  tm.init();
  tm.set(2);  //set brightness 0-7
}

void loop() {
  // put your main code here, to run repeatedly:
  // this code shows 12:34
```

```
  tm.display(0,1);
  tm.display(1,2);
  tm.point(1);
  tm.display(2,3);
  tm.display(3,4);
}
```

The following code generates and displays four-digit random numbers on the TM1637. CLK, DIO, VCC, and GND pins of the TM1637 board are connected to pins 2, 3, +5, and GND of the Arduino board, respectively.

```
#include <TM1637.h>
int CLK=2;
int DIO=3;
int number=0;

TM1637 tm(CLK,DIO);

void setup() {
  // put your setup code here, to run once:
  tm.init();
  tm.set(2); //set brightness 0-7
  randomSeed(analogRead(0));
  delay(500);
}

void loop() {
  // put your main code here, to run repeatedly:
  // this code generates a random number between 1000-9999 and
     displays it
  number=random(1000,9999);
  displayNumber(number);
  delay(1000);
}
```

```
void displayNumber(int num){
    tm.display(3, num % 10);
    tm.display(2, num / 10 % 10);
    tm.display(1, num / 100 % 10);
    tm.display(0, num / 1000 % 10);
}
```

2.17 Reading Digital Data

In this example, we will use a push button to turn on the onboard LED. Upload the following code to the board:

```
int pushButton=9;

void setup() {
  // put your setup code here, to run once:
  pinMode(LED_BUILTIN,OUTPUT);
  pinMode(pushButton,INPUT);
}

void loop() {
  // put your main code here, to run repeatedly:
  digitalWrite(LED_BUILTIN,digitalRead(pushButton));
}
```

The hardware of this example is shown in Figure 2-37. When you press the push button, +5 V reaches pin 9, and the digitalRead function returns 1. This turns on the onboard LED. The digitalRead returns 0 when the push button is not pressed because pin 9 is connected to ground through a 10 kΩ resistor. The onboard LED is off when digitalRead returns 0.

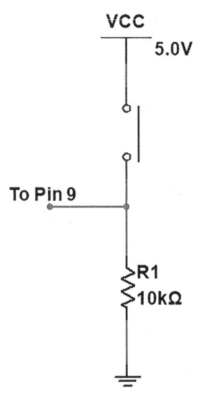

Figure 2-37. *A button is connected to the board with the aid of a pull-down resistor*

Change the hardware to what is shown in Figure 2-38. This time, the onboard LED turns off when you press the push button. Why?

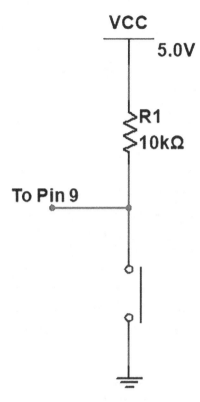

Figure 2-38. *A button is connected to the board with the aid of a pull-up resistor*

2.18 Internal Pull-Up Resistor

The microcontroller used on the Arduino board has internal pull-up resistors which can be activated with coding. If you activate the internal pull-up resistors, then there is no need to add them externally.

The following code shows how to activate the pull-up resistor of pin 9. Upload the code to the board:

```
const int LED=LED_BUILTIN;
const int pushButton=9;
```

```
int value=0;

void setup() {
  // put your setup code here, to run once:
  pinMode(LED,OUTPUT);
  pinMode(pushButton,INPUT_PULLUP);
}

void loop() {
  // put your main code here, to run repeatedly:
  value=digitalRead(pushButton);
  digitalWrite(LED_BUILTIN,!value);
}
```

The code activates the internal resistor of pin 9. Therefore, there is no need to add an external pull-up resistor. The hardware of this example is shown in Figure 2-39. As shown in Figure 2-40, the pull-up resistor inside the microcontroller is activated.

Figure 2-39. *A button is connected to pin 9 of the Arduino board*

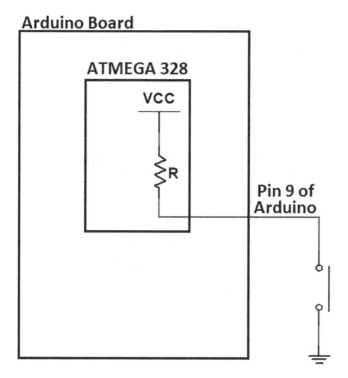

Figure 2-40. *The internal pull-up resistor of the microcontroller is activated*

When you press the push button, the onboard LED turns on. When you release it, the onboard LED turns off.

2.19 Toggle a Pin

This example does the same job as the one shown in Section 2.6. After uploading the code to the board, the onboard LED starts to blink.

```
void setup() {
  // put your setup code here, to run once:
  pinMode(LED_BUILTIN,OUTPUT);
}
```

89

```
void loop() {
  // put your main code here, to run repeatedly:
  digitalWrite(LED_BUILTIN,!digitalRead(LED_BUILTIN));
  delay(1000);
}
```

2.20 One-Digit Decimal Counter

In this example, we will make a decimal counter which counts from zero to nine. The output of the counter is shown on a seven-segment display. Two buttons control the output of the counter: one button increases the output, and the other button decreases it. Upload the following code to the board:

```
const int a=2;
const int b=3;
const int c=4;
const int d=5;
const int e=6;
const int f=7;
const int g=8;
const int dec=9;
const int inc=10;
int value=0;
void displayNumber(int n);
void clearDisp();

void setup() {
  pinMode(a,OUTPUT);
  pinMode(b,OUTPUT);
  pinMode(c,OUTPUT);
  pinMode(d,OUTPUT);
  pinMode(e,OUTPUT);
```

```
  pinMode(f,OUTPUT);
  pinMode(g,OUTPUT);
  pinMode(dec,INPUT);
  pinMode(inc,INPUT);
}

void loop() {
  // put your main code here, to run repeatedly:
  if (digitalRead(dec)==LOW){
    delay(300);
    value=value-1;
    if (value<0)
      value=0;
  }

  if (digitalRead(inc)==LOW){
    delay(300);
    value=value+1;
    if (value>9)
      value=9;
  }

  displayNumber(value);
}

void clearDisp(){
  digitalWrite(a,LOW);
  digitalWrite(b,LOW);
  digitalWrite(c,LOW);
  digitalWrite(d,LOW);
  digitalWrite(e,LOW);
  digitalWrite(f,LOW);
  digitalWrite(g,LOW);
}
```

```
void displayNumber(int n)
{
switch (n){
  case 0:
  clearDisp();
  digitalWrite(a,HIGH);
  digitalWrite(b,HIGH);
  digitalWrite(c,HIGH);
  digitalWrite(d,HIGH);
  digitalWrite(e,HIGH);
  digitalWrite(f,HIGH);
  digitalWrite(g,LOW);
    break;

  case 1:
  clearDisp();
  digitalWrite(a,LOW);
  digitalWrite(b,HIGH);
  digitalWrite(c,HIGH);
  digitalWrite(d,LOW);
  digitalWrite(e,LOW);
  digitalWrite(f,LOW);
  digitalWrite(g,LOW);
    break;

  case 2:
  clearDisp();
  digitalWrite(a,HIGH);
  digitalWrite(b,HIGH);
  digitalWrite(c,LOW);
  digitalWrite(d,HIGH);
  digitalWrite(e,HIGH);
```

```
digitalWrite(f,LOW);
digitalWrite(g,HIGH);
  break;

case 3:
clearDisp();
digitalWrite(a,HIGH);
digitalWrite(b,HIGH);
digitalWrite(c,HIGH);
digitalWrite(d,HIGH);
digitalWrite(e,LOW);
digitalWrite(f,LOW);
digitalWrite(g,HIGH);
  break;

case 4:
clearDisp();
digitalWrite(a,LOW);
digitalWrite(b,HIGH);
digitalWrite(c,HIGH);
digitalWrite(d,LOW);
digitalWrite(e,LOW);
digitalWrite(f,HIGH);
digitalWrite(g,HIGH);
  break;

case 5:
clearDisp();
digitalWrite(a,HIGH);
digitalWrite(b,LOW);
digitalWrite(c,HIGH);
```

```
digitalWrite(d,HIGH);
digitalWrite(e,LOW);
digitalWrite(f,HIGH);
digitalWrite(g,HIGH);
  break;

case 6:
clearDisp();
digitalWrite(a,HIGH);
digitalWrite(b,LOW);
digitalWrite(c,HIGH);
digitalWrite(d,HIGH);
digitalWrite(e,HIGH);
digitalWrite(f,HIGH);
digitalWrite(g,HIGH);
  break;

case 7:
clearDisp();
digitalWrite(a,HIGH);
digitalWrite(b,HIGH);
digitalWrite(c,HIGH);
digitalWrite(d,LOW);
digitalWrite(e,LOW);
digitalWrite(f,LOW);
digitalWrite(g,LOW);
  break;
```

```
case 8:
clearDisp();
digitalWrite(a,HIGH);
digitalWrite(b,HIGH);
digitalWrite(c,HIGH);
digitalWrite(d,HIGH);
digitalWrite(e,HIGH);
digitalWrite(f,HIGH);
digitalWrite(g,HIGH);
    break;

case 9:
clearDisp();
digitalWrite(a,HIGH);
digitalWrite(b,HIGH);
digitalWrite(c,HIGH);
digitalWrite(d,HIGH);
digitalWrite(e,LOW);
digitalWrite(f,HIGH);
digitalWrite(g,HIGH);
    break;
}
}
```

The hardware of this example is shown in Figure 2-41.

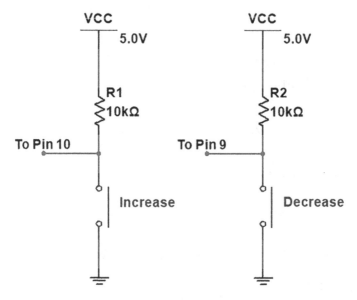

Figure 2-41. *Hardware of the studied example*

2.21 Electronic Dice

In this example, we want to make a digital dice. The output of this example is a random number between one and six. The output is shown on a common cathode seven-segment display. Upload the following code to the board:

```
const int a=2;
const int b=3;
const int c=4;
const int d=5;
const int e=6;
const int f=7;
const int g=8;
const int pushButton=9;
int value=0;
```

```
void displayNumber(int n);
void clearDisp();

void setup() {
  pinMode(a,OUTPUT);
  pinMode(b,OUTPUT);
  pinMode(c,OUTPUT);
  pinMode(d,OUTPUT);
  pinMode(e,OUTPUT);
  pinMode(f,OUTPUT);
  pinMode(g,OUTPUT);
  pinMode(pushButton,INPUT_PULLUP);
  digitalWrite(a,HIGH);
  digitalWrite(b,HIGH);
  digitalWrite(c,HIGH);
  digitalWrite(d,HIGH);
  digitalWrite(e,HIGH);
  digitalWrite(f,HIGH);
  digitalWrite(g,LOW);
  randomSeed(analogRead(0));
}

void loop() {
  // put your main code here, to run repeatedly:
  value=digitalRead(pushButton);
  if (value==LOW){
    delay(250);
    displayNumber(random(7));
  }
}
```

```
void clearDisp(){
  digitalWrite(a,LOW);
  digitalWrite(b,LOW);
  digitalWrite(c,LOW);
  digitalWrite(d,LOW);
  digitalWrite(e,LOW);
  digitalWrite(f,LOW);
  digitalWrite(g,LOW);
}

void displayNumber(int n)
{
switch (n){
  case 1:
  clearDisp();
  delay(100);
  digitalWrite(a,LOW);
  digitalWrite(b,HIGH);
  digitalWrite(c,HIGH);
  digitalWrite(d,LOW);
  digitalWrite(e,LOW);
  digitalWrite(f,LOW);
  digitalWrite(g,LOW);
    break;

  case 2:
  clearDisp();
  delay(100);
  digitalWrite(a,HIGH);
  digitalWrite(b,HIGH);
  digitalWrite(c,LOW);
  digitalWrite(d,HIGH);
```

```
digitalWrite(e,HIGH);
digitalWrite(f,LOW);
digitalWrite(g,HIGH);
  break;

case 3:
clearDisp();
delay(100);
digitalWrite(a,HIGH);
digitalWrite(b,HIGH);
digitalWrite(c,HIGH);
digitalWrite(d,HIGH);
digitalWrite(e,LOW);
digitalWrite(f,LOW);
digitalWrite(g,HIGH);
  break;

case 4:
clearDisp();
delay(100);
digitalWrite(a,LOW);
digitalWrite(b,HIGH);
digitalWrite(c,HIGH);
digitalWrite(d,LOW);
digitalWrite(e,LOW);
digitalWrite(f,HIGH);
digitalWrite(g,HIGH);
  break;

case 5:
clearDisp();
delay(100);
digitalWrite(a,HIGH);
```

```
digitalWrite(b,LOW);
digitalWrite(c,HIGH);
digitalWrite(d,HIGH);
digitalWrite(e,LOW);
digitalWrite(f,HIGH);
digitalWrite(g,HIGH);
   break;

case 6:
clearDisp();
delay(100);
digitalWrite(a,HIGH);
digitalWrite(b,LOW);
digitalWrite(c,HIGH);
digitalWrite(d,HIGH);
digitalWrite(e,HIGH);
digitalWrite(f,HIGH);
digitalWrite(g,HIGH);
   break;
}
}
```

The hardware of this example is shown in Figure 2-42. When you press the push button, a random number is displayed on the seven-segment display.

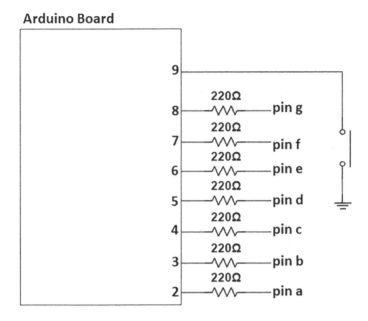

Figure 2-42. *Hardware of the studied example*

2.22 Reading a Keypad

In this section, we will see how a keypad can be read with the aid of a Keypad library. The schematic of a typical keypad is shown in Figure 2-43. This keypad has four rows and four columns.

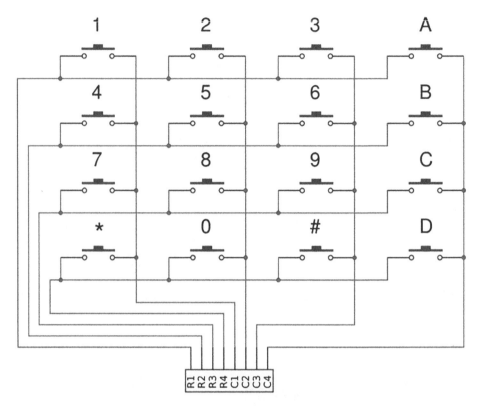

Figure 2-43. *Schematic of a typical keyboard*

The following code shows how to read a keyboard with the aid of a Keypad library:

```
#include <Keypad.h>

const byte ROWS = 4; //four rows
const byte COLS = 4; //three columns
char keys[ROWS][COLS] = {
  {'1','2','3','A'},
  {'4','5','6','B'},
  {'7','8','9','C'},
  {'*','0','#','D'}
};
```

```
byte rowPins[ROWS] = {5, 4, 3, 2}; //connect to the row pinouts
of the keypad
byte colPins[COLS] = {9, 8, 7, 6}; //connect to the column
pinouts of the keypad

Keypad keypad = Keypad( makeKeymap(keys), rowPins, colPins,
ROWS, COLS );

void setup(){
  Serial.begin(9600);
}

void loop(){
  char key = keypad.getKey();

  if (key != NO_KEY){
    Serial.println(key);
  }
}
```

Hardware connections are shown in Table 2-6.

Table 2-6. *Connections between Arduino and the keypad*

Keypad Pin	Arduino Pin
R4	2
R3	3
R2	4
R1	5
C4	6
C3	7
C2	8
C1	9

After uploading the code to the board, click Tools ➤ Serial Monitor in order to see the result. When you press the keypad keys, they are shown in the Serial Monitor window.

2.23 Simple Calculator

In this example, we want to make a simple calculator. The keypad of this calculator is shown in Figure 2-44.

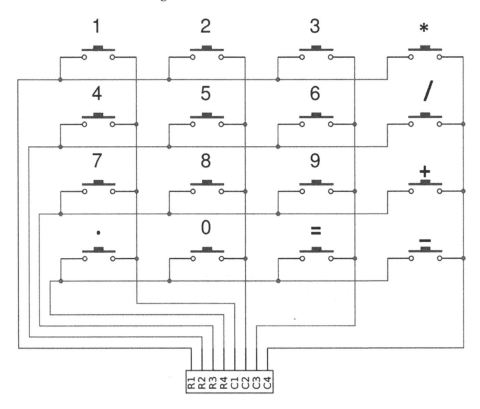

Figure 2-44. *Schematic of a keypad used in the example*

Upload the following code to the board:

```
#include <Keypad.h>
String num1="",num2="";
String operation="";
float result=0.0;

const byte ROWS = 4; //four rows
const byte COLS = 4; //three columns
char keys[ROWS][COLS] = {
  {'1','2','3','*'},
  {'4','5','6','/'},
  {'7','8','9','+'},
  {'.','0','=','-'}
};
byte rowPins[ROWS] = {5, 4, 3, 2}; //connect to the row pinouts
of the keypad
byte colPins[COLS] = {9, 8, 7, 6}; //connect to the column
pinouts of the keypad

Keypad keypad = Keypad( makeKeymap(keys), rowPins, colPins,
ROWS, COLS );

void setup(){
  Serial.begin(9600);
}

void loop(){
  char key = keypad.getKey();

  if (key!=NO_KEY&& key=='C'){
    num1="";
    num2="";
    operation="";
    result=0;
  }
```

```
if (key != NO_KEY&& operation==""&& (key=='1'||key=='2'||
key=='3'||key=='4'||key=='5'||key=='6'||key=='7'||key=='8'||
key=='9'||key=='0'||key=='.')){
  Serial.print(key);
  num1=num1+key;
}

if(key != NO_KEY&& (key=='+'||key=='-'||key=='*'||key=='/')){
  Serial.print(key);
  operation=key;
}

if (key != NO_KEY&& operation!=""&& (key=='1'||key=='2'||
key=='3'||key=='4'||key=='5'||key=='6'||key=='7'||key=='8'||
key=='9'||key=='0'||key=='.')){
  Serial.print(key);
  num2=num2+key;
}

if (key != NO_KEY&& (key=='=')){
    if (operation=="*"){
      result=num1.toFloat()*num2.toFloat();
      Serial.println((String)"="+result);
      num1="";
      num2="";
      operation="";
      result=0;
    }

    if (operation=="/"){
      result=num1.toFloat()/num2.toFloat();
      Serial.println((String)"="+result);
      num1="";
```

```
      num2="";
      operation="";
      result=0;
    }

    if (operation=="+"){
      result=num1.toFloat()+num2.toFloat();
      Serial.println((String)"="+result);
      num1="";
      num2="";
      operation="";
      result=0;
    }

    if (operation=="-"){
      result=num1.toFloat()-num2.toFloat();
      Serial.println((String)"="+result);
      num1="";
      num2="";
      operation="";
      result=0;
    }
  }

  delay(50);
}
```

Hardware connections are shown in Table 2-7.

Table 2-7. *Connections between*
Arduino and the keypad

Keypad Pin	Arduino Pin
R4	2
R3	3
R2	4
R1	5
C4	6
C3	7
C2	8
C1	9

After uploading the code to the board, click Tools ➤ Serial Monitor in order to see the result. Use the = key to see the result (Figure 2-45).

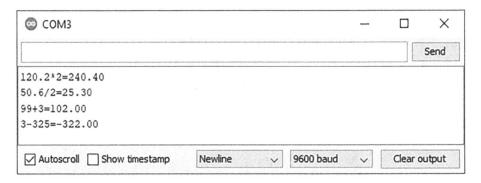

Figure 2-45. *Sample output*

2.24 Simple Digital Lock

In this example, we want to make a simple digital lock. The user enters the password and presses the # key in order to check it. If the entered password is correct, then a "Correct Password..." message will be shown on the screen, and the onboard LED lights up. The keypad of this example is shown in Figure 2-46. Connection between the Arduino board and the keypad is shown in Table 2-8.

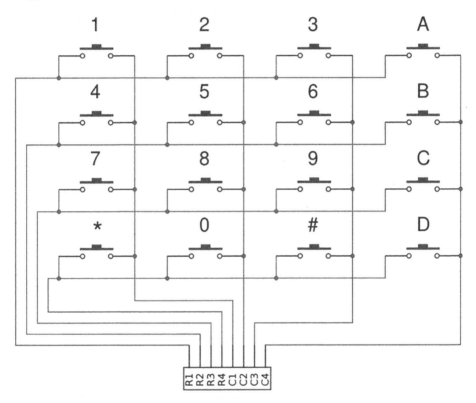

Figure 2-46. *Schematic of the keypad used in the example*

```
#include <Keypad.h>
String code="";
const int password="12A7";
```

```
const byte ROWS = 4; //four rows
const byte COLS = 4; //three columns
char keys[ROWS][COLS] = {
  {'1','2','3','A'},
  {'4','5','6','B'},
  {'7','8','9','C'},
  {'*','0','#','D'}
};
byte rowPins[ROWS] = {5, 4, 3, 2}; //connect to the row pinouts
of the keypad
byte colPins[COLS] = {9, 8, 7, 6}; //connect to the column
pinouts of the keypad

Keypad keypad = Keypad( makeKeymap(keys), rowPins, colPins,
ROWS, COLS );

void setup(){
  Serial.begin(9600);
  pinMode(LED_BUILTIN,OUTPUT);
  digitalWrite(LED_BUILTIN,LOW);
  Serial.print("Enter your password: ");
}

void loop(){
  char key = keypad.getKey();

  if (key != NO_KEY&& (key=='1'||key=='2'||key=='3'||key=='4'
                              ||key=='5'||key=='6'||key=='7'
                              ||key=='8'||key=='9'||key=='0'
                              ||key=='A'||key=='B'||key=='C'
                              ||key=='D'||key=='E')){

    code=code+key;
    Serial.print(key);
  }
```

```
  if(key != NO_KEY&& key=='#'){
    if (code==password){
        digitalWrite(LED_BUILTIN,HIGH);
        Serial.print("\nCorrect Password...");
    }else{
        Serial.print("\nWrong Password...");
        code="";
        Serial.print("\nEnter your password: ");
    }
  }

  delay(50);
}
```

Table 2-8. *Connections between*
Arduino and the keypad

Keypad Pin	Arduino Pin
R4	2
R3	3
R2	4
R1	5
C4	6
C3	7
C2	8
C1	9

After uploading the code to the board, click Tools ➤ Serial Monitor in
order to see the result.

111

2.25 Switch Bouncing and How to Avoid It

When we press a push button, two metal parts come into contact to short the supply. They don't connect instantly, but the metal parts connect and disconnect several times before the actual stable connection is made. The same thing happens while releasing the button. This results in the false triggering or multiple triggering like the button is pressed multiple times. It's like dropping a ball from a height, and it keeps bouncing on the surface until it comes to rest.

The bouncing problem can be solved using software or hardware approaches. This section focuses on the hardware approach. A simple RC debouncing is shown in Figure 2-47. Diode D is optional and it can be removed (you can use 1N4148). Typical values of resistor R and capacitor C are 10 kΩ and 1 µF.

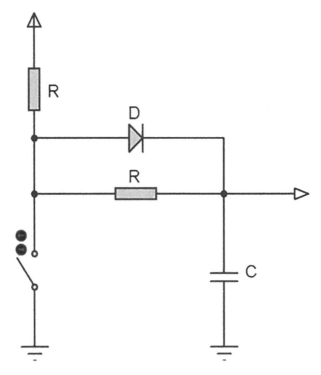

Figure 2-47. *RC debouncing circuit*

There are ICs available in the market for switch debouncing. Some of the debouncing ICs are MAX6816, MC14490, and LS118. For instance, debouncing with the aid of MAX6816 is shown in Figure 2-48.

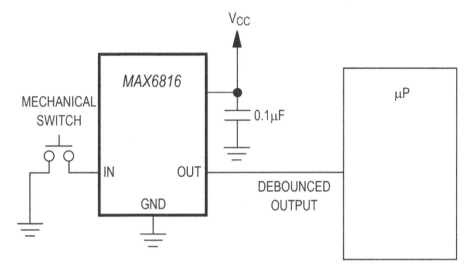

Figure 2-48. *Debouncing with MAX6816*

2.26 Implementation of Logic Functions

The implementation of logic functions is studied in this section. Table 2-9 shows different logic operations and their C language equivalent.

Table 2-9. *Logic operations and their C language equivalent*

Operation	C Language Equivalent
AND	&
OR	|
XOR	^
NOT	!
Shift Right	>>
Shift Left	<<

Let's study an example. Assume that we want to write a code to implement the F=A.(B+C)! The truth table of this function is shown in Table 2-10.

Table 2-10. *Truth table for F=A.(B+C)'*

A	B	C	F
0	0	0	0
0	0	1	0
0	1	0	0
0	1	1	0
1	0	0	1
1	0	1	0
1	1	0	0
1	1	1	0

The following code implements the given logic function. Inputs A, B, and C are entered into pins 2, 3, and 4. The output is taken from pin 13. The onboard LED of Arduino UNO is connected to pin 13. Therefore, the onboard LED shows the output.

```
#define Apin 2
#define Bpin 3
#define Cpin 4
#define Fpin 13

int A=0;
int B=0;
int C=0;
int F=0;

void setup() {
  // put your setup code here, to run once:
  pinMode(Apin,INPUT);
  pinMode(Bpin,INPUT);
  pinMode(Cpin,INPUT);
  pinMode(Fpin,OUTPUT);
}

void loop() {
  // put your main code here, to run repeatedly:
  A=digitalRead(Apin);
  B=digitalRead(Bpin);
  C=digitalRead(Cpin);
  F=A&(!(B|C));
  digitalWrite(Fpin,F);
}
```

The hardware of this example is shown in Figure 2-49. Test the circuit and ensure that it implements the truth table shown in Table 2-10.

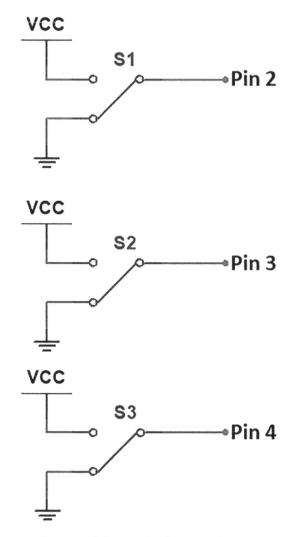

Figure 2-49. *Hardware of the studied example*

2.27 Bit Shift Operators

The left shift operator << causes the bits of the left operand to be shifted left by the number of positions specified by the right operand. For example, assume that A=5. The binary equivalent of variable A is 101. A<<3 gives 101000 or 40 in decimal. Note that a left shift by n positions is equal to multiplying by 2^n.

The right shift operator >> causes the bits of the left operand to be shifted right by the number of positions specified by the right operand. For example, assume B=41. The binary equivalent of variable B is 101001. B>>3 gives 101 or 8 in decimal. Note that a right shift by n positions is equal to division by 2^n.

The following code helps you to understand how these operators work. Upload the code to the board:

```
int a=0;

void setup() {
  // put your setup code here, to run once:
  Serial.begin(9600);
}

void loop() {
  // put your main code here, to run repeatedly:
  int n=0b101101;
  Serial.println("n is a binary number with value of 101101.");
  for (int i=1;i<=6;i++){
    a=n>>i;
    Serial.print((String)"Result of n>>"+i+" is ");
    Serial.println(a,BIN);
  }
  Serial.println("-------");

  Serial.println("n is a binary number with value of 101101.");
```

```
for (int i=1;i<=6;i++){
  a=n<<i;
  Serial.print((String)"Result of n<<"+i+" is ");
  Serial.println(a,BIN);
}
Serial.println("-------");

delay(120000);
}
```

After uploading the code, open the Serial Monitor (Tools ➤ Serial Monitor) to see the output of the code.

2.28 Logical Bitwise Operations

Logical bitwise operations permit you to do the desired logical operation on corresponding bits of two operands. For example, assume that A=178 and B=150. The binary equivalents of these two variables are A=10110010 and B=10010110.

Tables 2-11 and 2-12 show the result of different bitwise operations on the given two variables.

Table 2-11. *Result of bitwise AND between A and B*

A	1	0	1	1	0	0	1	0
B	1	0	0	1	0	1	1	0
A&B	1	0	0	1	0	0	1	0

Table 2-12. *Result of bitwise OR between A and B*

A	1	0	1	1	0	0	1	0
B	1	0	0	1	0	1	1	0
A|B	**1**	**0**	**1**	**1**	**0**	**1**	**1**	**0**

Bitwise negation takes only one operand. For instance, ~A=01001101 and ~B=01101001.

The following code helps you to understand how logical bitwise operators work. Upload the code to the board:

```
byte a=0b10110010; //in decimal: 178
byte b=0b10010110; //in decimal: 150
byte c=0;
byte d=0;

void setup() {
  // put your setup code here, to run once:
  Serial.begin(9600);
}

void loop() {
  // put your main code here, to run repeatedly:
  Serial.println((String)"a=10110010="+a+", b=10010110="+b);
  Serial.println("");

  c=~a;
  d=~b;
  Serial.print("~a=");
  Serial.println(c,BIN);
  Serial.print("~b=");
  Serial.println(d,BIN);
  Serial.println("");
```

```
c=a&b;
d=a|b;
Serial.print((String)"a&b=10110010&10010110=");
Serial.print(c,BIN);
Serial.println((String)", in decimal= "+c);
Serial.println("");

Serial.print((String)"a|b=10110010|10010110=");
Serial.print(d,BIN);
Serial.println((String)", in decimal= "+d);

Serial.println("-------------------------------------------");
delay(60000);
}
```

After uploading the code, open the Serial Monitor (Tools ➤ Serial Monitor) to see the output of the code.

2.29 Setting and Clearing a Specific Bit

You change the bits of a variable as well. For instance, assume that A=178, which is equal to 10110010 in binary. The MSB (leftmost bit) of A is 1. With the aid of bitClear(A,7), you can make the MSB of A zero. Therefore, after running the command bitClear(A,7), the value of A will be 00110010, which is equal to 50 in decimal. The bitClear(A,n) command writes 0 to the nth bit of variable A. n starts at 0 for the least significant (rightmost) bit.

You can use the bitSet command in order to make a bit 1. The following code helps you to understand how bitSet and bitClear commands work:

```
byte a=178; // Binary representation of 178 is 10110010.
byte b=0;
byte c=0;
```

```
void setup() {
  // put your setup code here, to run once:
  Serial.begin(9600);
}

void loop() {
  // put your main code here, to run repeatedly:
  Serial.println("a=178=10110010");
  Serial.println();

  for (int i=sizeof(a)*8-1;i>=0;i--){
    Serial.println((String)"bit "+i+ " of a is: "+bitRead(a,i)) ;
  }

  Serial.println();
  b=bitSet(a,6);
  Serial.println((String)"bitSet(a,6)="+b); //11110010=242 is
  expected.

  c=bitClear(b,6);
  Serial.println((String)"bitClear(b,6)="+c); //10110010=178 is
  expected.

  delay(60000);
}
```

After uploading the code, open the Serial Monitor (Tools ➤ Serial Monitor) to see the output of the code.

2.30 Control a Buzzer with Arduino

A buzzer is a basic audio device that generates a sound from an incoming electrical signal. The following code shows how to make a sound with a buzzer. In the following code, the buzzer makes a sound for 500 ms, then becomes silent for 3 s, and this cycle repeats. Upload the code to the board:

```
void setup() {
  pinMode(9,OUTPUT);
}

void loop() {
  // put your main code here, to run repeatedly:
  tone(9,900); // 900 Hz on pin 9, duty cycle 50%
  delay(500);
  noTone(9);
  delay(3000);
}
```

The hardware of this example is shown in Figure 2-50.

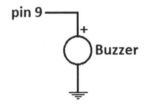

Figure 2-50. *Hardware of the studied example*

2.31 Control a Relay with Arduino

A relay is an electromechanical switch, and it is suitable for connecting or disconnecting heavy loads (i.e., loads that require high currents). The following circuit shows how a relay can be connected to a microcontroller. When a microcontroller pin generates +5 V, the transistor is on and the relay is activated. In this case, the electromagnet inside the relay connects the common pin C to the normally open (NO) pin. When the microcontroller pin generates 0 V, the transistor is off and the electromagnet inside the relay is not activated. In this case, the spring inside the relay connects the common pin C to the normally closed (NC) pin. The diode 1N4001 in Figure 2-51 protects the transistor and is necessary. The circuit shown in Figure 2-51 works with most of the relays. If it doesn't work with your relay, then you can decrease the 510 Ω resistor.

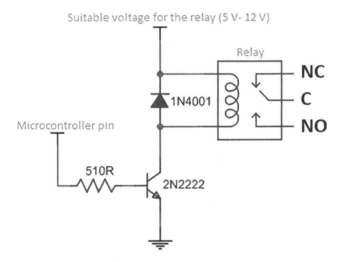

Figure 2-51. *Connecting a relay to a microcontroller pin*

Let's assume that for some reason the collector of a transistor is shorted to the base as shown in Figure 2-52. In this case, the voltage that supplies the relay can reach the microcontroller pin, and it may destroy the microcontroller pin (this happens especially when the relay voltage is high). Therefore, the schematic shown in Figure 2-51 works; however, from an isolation point of view, it is not a good solution. Let's try to solve the isolation problem.

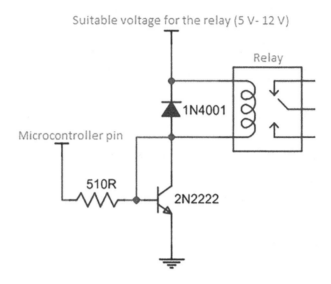

Figure 2-52. *The collector is connected to the base*

Figure 2-53 shows a circuit which uses the optocoupler. The optocoupler isolates the microcontroller pin from the relay completely. The microcontroller signal is sent to the transistor with the aid of the light that the LED generates. The schematic shown in Figure 2-53 is a better solution in comparison to Figure 2-51. You can decrease the 510 Ω resistor if the relay is not activated when the microcontroller pin is high.

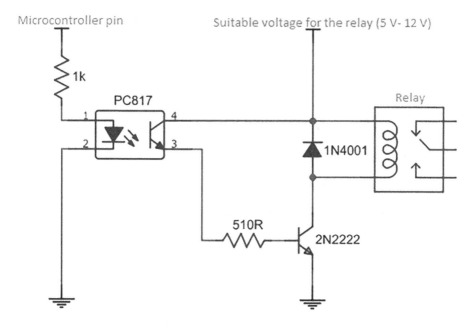

Microcontroller pin

Suitable voltage for the relay (5 V- 12 V)

1k

PC817

Relay

1N4001

510R

2N2222

Figure 2-53. *An optocoupler isolates the microcontroller from the*
rest of the system

Let's see how the circuit shown in Figure 2-53 works. When the microcontroller pin is high, the LED sends a light to the phototransistor, and the voltage drop between pins 3 and 4 in Figure 2-53 becomes around 0 V. This permits the base current to pass. The base current forces the transistor to go into the saturation, and the relay is activated. When the microcontroller pin is low, the LED doesn't generate any light, and the phototransistor acts as an open circuit and stops the base current. When the base current is around zero, the transistor goes into cutoff, and the relay is turned off.

2.32 References for Further Study

[1]   Definition of digital signals:

https://bit.ly/3VoJbi6

[2]   Digital pins of Arduino:

https://bit.ly/3PT9fAy

[3]   Definition of hysteresis:

https://bit.ly/3VFr2wF

[4]   Applications of 74HC595:

https://bit.ly/3jrt6L8

https://bit.ly/3I1D3ZW

[5]   Debouncing:

https://bit.ly/3hVJOBV

[6]   TM1637 four-digit display:

https://bit.ly/3jw6WaE

[7]   Keypad:

https://bit.ly/3WrQ6rU

https://bit.ly/3Wrhu9o

CHAPTER 3

Analog-to-Digital Converter (ADC) and Digital-to-Analog Converter (DAC)

3.1 Introduction

In the previous chapter, you learned how to read and generate digital signals. This chapter shows how you can read and generate analog signals. Digital systems can generate or read analog signals with the aid of two building blocks: digital-to-analog converter and analog-to-digital converter. These two building blocks are introduced as follows.

A digital-to-analog converter (DAC, D/A, or D-to-A) is a system that converts a digital signal into an analog signal. Arduino UNO doesn't have an onboard DAC. If your project requires a DAC, you need to add it externally.

An analog-to-digital converter (ADC, A/D, or A-to-D) is a system that converts an analog signal, such as a sound picked up by a microphone or light entering a digital camera, into a digital signal. The microcontrollers

© Farzin Asadi 2023
F. Asadi, *Essentials of Arduino™ Boards Programming*, Maker Innovations Series,
https://doi.org/10.1007/978-1-4842-9600-4_3

used in Arduino boards have an onboard ADC. Therefore, there is no need
to add an external ADC to the board.

In Arduino UNO, analog signals can be entered into pins A0, A1, A2,
A3, A4, and A5 (Figure 3-1). Arduino UNO has a 10-bit ADC. Therefore, the
ADC output changes from 0000000000 up to 1111111111 (from 0 to 1023).
Input impedance of the ADC is around 100 MΩ.

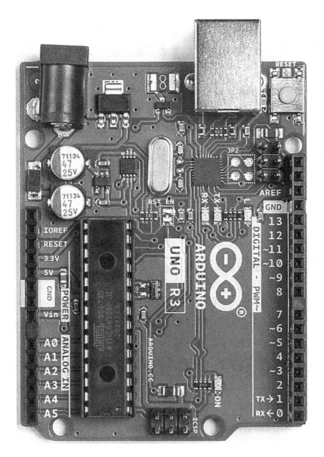

Figure 3-1. *Arduino UNO board*

The AREF (Analog Reference) pin (see the top-right side of Figure 3-1) can be used to provide an external reference voltage for the analog-to-digital conversion of inputs to the analog pins. The reference voltage essentially specifies the value for the top of the input range and consequently each discrete step in the converted output. When the AREF pin is not connected to anywhere, the reference voltage is +5 V.

If we show the reference voltage and output of the ADC with VREF and N, respectively, then the analog voltage applied to the analog pin is $N/1023 \times VREF$. Let's study an example. Assume that the ADC reads 0111011100 and AREF is not connected to any external reference voltage. In this case, the reference voltage is 5 V, and the analog voltage applied to the analog pin is $476/1023 \times 5 = 2.326$ V. Note that $(0111011100)_2 = (476)_{10}$.

As another example, assume that the output of the ADC is 1000110011 and the AREF pin is connected to 1.1 V. In this case, the analog voltage applied to the analog pin is $563/1023 \times 1.1 = 0.605$ V. Note that $(1000110011)_2 = (563)_{10}$.

3.2 Protection of ADC

The ADC cannot accept negative voltages and voltages bigger than +5 V. Therefore, it is a good idea to protect the ADC against voltages outside the allowed range. The simplest protection is shown in Figure 3-2. When the input voltage is bigger than 5 V, the Zener diode enters into the breakdown region, and the voltage that reaches the analog pin keeps constant at around +5 V. The Zener diode becomes forward bias when negative voltages are applied. In this case, the voltage of the analog pin is around –0.7 V. If you put a Schottky diode in parallel with the Zener diode (Figure 3-3), this value decreases to around –0.2 V.

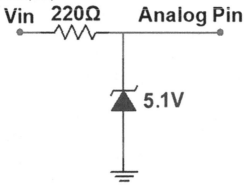

Figure 3-2. Protection of the ADC with a Zener diode

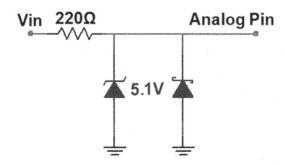

*Figure 3-3. Protection of the ADC with a Zener diode and a
Schottky diode*

You can use a voltage divider to measure the voltages bigger than 5 V.
For instance, the voltage divider in Figure 3-4 has an attenuation ratio of
$\frac{100}{100+220} = 0.312$. This circuit can be used to measure the voltages up
to 16 V. The Zener diode protects the ADC against voltages bigger than 16 V.
You can put a Schottky diode in parallel with the Zener diode as well in
order to make a better protection against negative voltages.

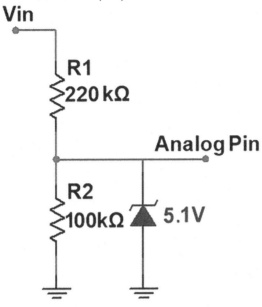

Figure 3-4. *The voltage divider decreases the voltage that reaches
the ADC*

It is a good idea to filter the signal before applying the signal to the
ADC. For instance, assume that we know that our input signal is band
limited to 100 Hz. In this case, components more than 100 Hz are not
important for us and need to be removed. You can add a capacitor to the
voltage divider in order to make a simple low pass RC filter (Figure 3-5).
The cutoff frequency is given by $f = \dfrac{1}{2\pi RC}$ where $R = \dfrac{R_1 R_2}{R_1 + R_2}$. For instance,
assume that R=68.75 kΩ in Figure 3-5. For the cutoff frequency of 100 Hz, C
must be equal to 23.15 nF.

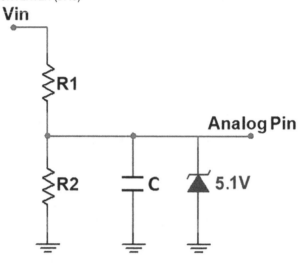

Figure 3-5. *Addition of a capacitor to the voltage divider*

3.3 Simple DC Voltmeter

In this example, you will make a simple DC voltmeter. This voltmeter
measures the voltages between 0 and +5 V. Upload the following code to
the board:

```
int analogPinA0=A0;
int value=0;
double Vref=5.0;

void setup() {
  // put your setup code here, to run once:
  Serial.begin(9600);
}

void loop() {
    value=analogRead(analogPinA0);

    double voltageA0=value*Vref/1023;
```

```
Serial.println((String)"Voltage given to ADC A0:
"+voltageA0);
Serial.println("------------------------------");
delay(3000);
}
```

The hardware of the example is shown in Figure 3-6. VCC and ground in this figure represent the +5 V and GND pins of the Arduino. The code measures the voltage of pin A0. You can apply a voltage between 0 and 5 V to pin A0 by rotating the knob of the potentiometer.

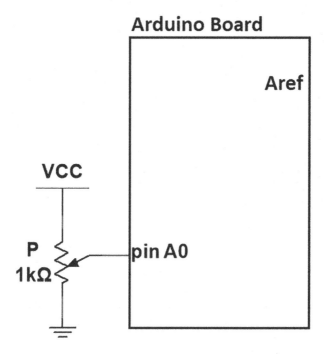

Figure 3-6. *Hardware of the studied example*

After uploading the code to the board, click Tools ➤ Serial Monitor in order to see the result. Connect a digital voltmeter to pin A0 and compare its reading with the output of the code.

3.4 Serial Plotter

The Serial Plotter is a very useful tool to graphically see the graph of a data that comes from the serial port. Let's see how the Serial Plotter works. Upload the following code to your board. This code sends two numbers to the computer: a random number and a constant number with a value of 500.

```
int random_variable;
int static_variable = 500;

void setup() {
  Serial.begin(9600);
}

void loop() {
  random_variable = random(0, 1000);

  Serial.print("Variable_1:");
  Serial.print(random_variable);
  Serial.print(",");
  Serial.print("Variable_2:");
  Serial.println(static_variable);
  delay(500);
}
```

After uploading the code, click Tools ➤ Serial Plotter. It starts to show the graph of data (Figure 3-7).

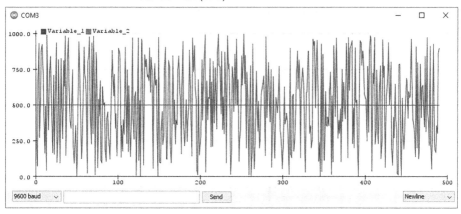

Figure 3-7. *Sample output*

Note that the unit of the horizontal axis is not time. The Serial Plotter is a simple tool which graphically shows the value(s) received from the serial port. A horizontal axis can be considered as the index of received data.

Let's use the Serial Plotter to see the graph of voltage that is applied to pin A0 of Arduino as well. Upload the following code to the board:

```
int analogPinA0=A0;
int value=0;
double Vref=5.08;

void setup() {
  // put your setup code here, to run once:
  Serial.begin(9600);
}

void loop() {
    value=analogRead(analogPinA0);

    double voltageA0=value*Vref/1023;
    Serial.println(voltageA0);
    delay(50);
}
```

The hardware of this example is shown in Figure 3-8. Rotate the potentiometer shaft; the Serial Plotter shows the changes of the voltage on the screen (Figure 3-9).

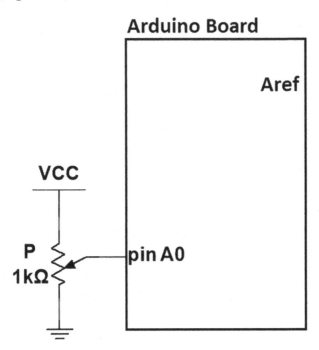

Figure 3-8. Hardware of the studied example

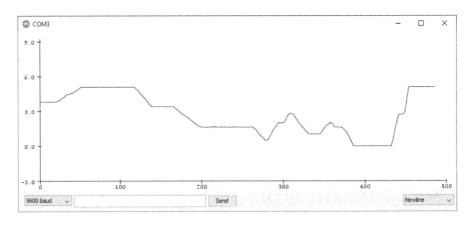

Figure 3-9. Sample output

3.5 AREF Pin

The AREF (Analog Reference) pin can be used to provide an external reference voltage for the analog-to-digital conversion of inputs to the analog pins. The reference voltage essentially specifies the value for the top of the input range and consequently each discrete step in the converted output. For instance, if you apply 3.3 V to the AREF pin, the analogRead returns 1023 for the input voltage of 3.3 V and 341 for the input voltage of 1.1 V. In this case, sensitivity is 3.3/1023= 3.2 mV. When no voltage is connected to the AREF pin, the reference voltage is 5 V.

Negative voltages and values bigger than 5 V cannot be applied to the AREF pin. If you're using an external reference on the AREF pin, you must set the analog reference to EXTERNAL before calling analogRead().

Let's make the simple voltmeter of Section 3.3 more accurate. Note that increasing the accuracy is achieved by decreasing the maximum of input voltage that is applicable to the ADC. Upload the following code to the board:

```
int analogPinA0=A0;
int value=0;
double Vref=3.3;

void setup() {
  // put your setup code here, to run once:
  Serial.begin(9600);
  analogReference(EXTERNAL);
}

void loop() {
    value=analogRead(analogPinA0);
```

```
    double voltageA0=value*Vref/1023;
    Serial.println((String)"Voltage given to ADC A0: "+voltageA0);
    Serial.println("-----------------------------");
    delay(3000);
}
```

The hardware of this example is shown in Figure 3-10. This voltmeter measures voltages between 0 and 3.3 V. Rotate the potentiometer shaft in order to change the voltage applied to pin A0. Use a digital voltmeter to measure the voltage applied to pin A0 and compare it with the value generated by the code.

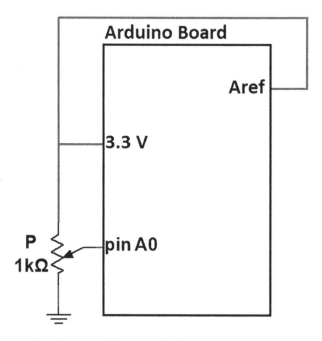

Figure 3-10. *Hardware of the studied example*

3.6 Speed of Conversion

The conversion from analog to digital takes some time. The following code measures this conversion time. Upload the code to the board:

```
//ADC
//On ATmega based boards (UNO, Nano, Mini, MEGA), it takes
about 100 microseconds
//to read an analog input, so the maximum reading rate is about
10,000 times a second.
//https://www.arduino.cc/reference/en/language/functions/
analog-io/analogread/

int analogPinA0=A0;
int value=0;
double Vref=5.0;

void setup() {
  // put your setup code here, to run once:
  Serial.begin(9600);
}

void loop() {
    double t0=micros();
    value=analogRead(analogPinA0);
    double t1=micros();
    int deltaT=t1-t0;

    Serial.println((String)"Value read from ADC A0: "+value);
    Serial.println();
    Serial.println((String)"Conversion time (us): "+deltaT);
    Serial.println();

    double voltageA0=value*Vref/1023;
```

```
    Serial.println((String)"Voltage given to ADC A0:
    "+voltageA0);
    Serial.println("------------------------------------");
    delay(3000);
}
```

The hardware of this example is shown in Figure 3-11. Open the Serial
Monitor (click Tools ➤ Serial Monitor) in order to observe the output of
the code. On Arduino UNO, it takes about 114 µs to convert one sample of
analog data into digital. Therefore, the maximum sampling frequency that
you can achieve is $f = \dfrac{1}{114\,\mu s} = 8.77\,kHz$. If you plan to send the digital data
to a computer using the serial port, you need to consider the time required
for transfer as well. For instance, in the preceding code, the variable value
which is an integer variable saves the conversion output. Integer variables
take 2 bytes, which is equal to 16 bits. Transferring 16 bits with a speed of
9600 bps takes 16 × 1/9600 = 1.67 ms (parity bits are ignored). Therefore,
the total time for conversion and transferring the data will be 114 µs + 1.67
ms = 1.78 ms.

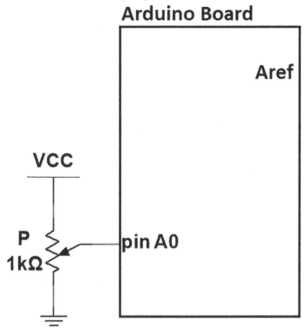

Figure 3-11. *Hardware of the studied example*

3.7 Voltage Level Indicator

In this section, we want to make a voltage level indicator. The hardware of this project is shown in Figure 3-12. VCC represents the +5 V pin of the Arduino board.

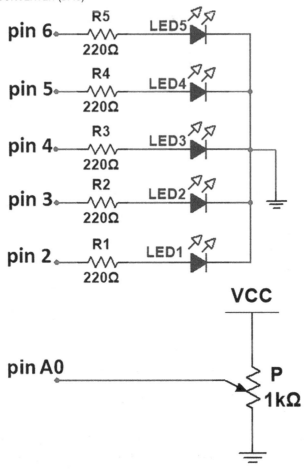

Figure 3-12. *Hardware of the studied example*

When the input voltage is between 0 and 1 V, LED 1 turns on; when
the input voltage is between 1 V and 2 V, LED 1 and LED 2 turn on; when
the input voltage is between 2 V and 3 V, LED 1, LED 2, and LED 3 turn on;
when the input voltage is between 3 V and 4 V, LED 1, LED 2, LED 3, and

LED 4 turn on; when the input voltage is between 4 V and 5 V, all of the
LEDs are turned on. Upload the code to the board:

```
int analogPin=A0;
double voltage=0;
double Vref=5.0;

const int LED1=2;
const int LED2=3;
const int LED3=4;
const int LED4=5;
const int LED5=6;

void setup() {
  // put your setup code here, to run once:
  pinMode(LED1,OUTPUT);
  pinMode(LED2,OUTPUT);
  pinMode(LED3,OUTPUT);
  pinMode(LED4,OUTPUT);
  pinMode(LED5,OUTPUT);
}

void loop() {
  // put your main code here, to run repeatedly:
  voltage=analogRead(analogPin)/1023.0*Vref;

  if (voltage>0.0 && voltage<=1.0){
    digitalWrite(LED1,HIGH);
    digitalWrite(LED2,LOW);
    digitalWrite(LED3,LOW);
    digitalWrite(LED4,LOW);
    digitalWrite(LED5,LOW);
  }
```

```
  if (voltage>1.0 && voltage<=2.0){
    digitalWrite(LED1,HIGH);
    digitalWrite(LED2,HIGH);
    digitalWrite(LED3,LOW);
    digitalWrite(LED4,LOW);
    digitalWrite(LED5,LOW);
  }

  if (voltage>2.0 && voltage<=3.0){
    digitalWrite(LED1,HIGH);
    digitalWrite(LED2,HIGH);
    digitalWrite(LED3,HIGH);
    digitalWrite(LED4,LOW);
    digitalWrite(LED5,LOW);
  }

  if (voltage>3.0 && voltage<=4.0){
    digitalWrite(LED1,HIGH);
    digitalWrite(LED2,HIGH);
    digitalWrite(LED3,HIGH);
    digitalWrite(LED4,HIGH);
    digitalWrite(LED5,LOW);
  }

  if (voltage>4.0 && voltage<=5.0){
    digitalWrite(LED1,HIGH);
    digitalWrite(LED2,HIGH);
    digitalWrite(LED3,HIGH);
    digitalWrite(LED4,HIGH);
    digitalWrite(LED5,HIGH);
  }

  delay(250);
}
```

3.8 Measurement of Negative Voltages

The ADC cannot measure negative voltages. One way to measure negative
voltages is to use a voltage divider. For instance, with the aid of a circuit
shown in Figure 3-13, you can measure the voltages in the [–12 V, +4.8 V]
interval.

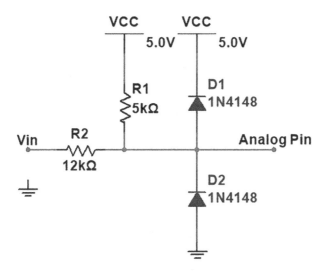

Figure 3-13. *A circuit to measure the voltages in the [–12 V, +4.8 V]
interval*

In Figure 3-13, the voltage that reaches the analog pin is
$0.294 \times Vin + 3.53$. For instance, when the analog pin senses 2 V, the input
voltage (Vin) is –5.2 V.

You can use a current mirror to measure negative voltages as well. For
instance, the DC transfer characteristic of the circuit shown in Figure 3-14
is shown in Figure 3-15. Note that this circuit pulls the negative inputs to
the positive range.

145

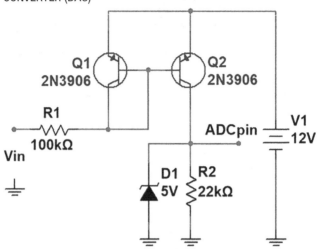

Figure 3-14. *Measurement of negative voltages with the current mirror*

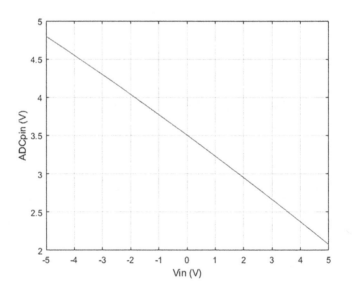

Figure 3-15. *DC transfer characteristic of the circuit shown in Figure 3-14*

In Figure 3-14, the voltage that reaches the analog pin is
$-0.271 \times Vin + 3.506$. For instance, when the analog pin senses 2 V, the input
voltage (Vin) is around +5 V.

Another technique to measure negative voltages can be found in the
references section.

3.9 Measurement of Current Signals

An ADC can measure voltage signals only. If you want to measure current
signals, you need to convert them into voltage signals first. The simplest
technique of converting a current signal into a voltage signal is by passing
the current signal through a series sense resistor. The voltage drop that
appears across the resistor linearly depends on the current passing
through it. This technique has some disadvantages. There is a power
dissipation in the resistor. The dissipated power increases the temperature
of the sense resistor. The change of temperature changes the value of the
sense resistor. Therefore, the I-V relation for this conversion technique may
not be quite linear.

Hall Effect sensors can be used to convert a current signal into a
voltage signal as well. In this section, we will make an ammeter with the
ACS712 current sensor. The ACS712 current sensor is a product of Allegro
MicroSystems that can be used for precise measurement of both AC and
DC currents. This sensor is based on the Hall Effect, and the IC has an
integrated Hall Effect device. The breakout board of ACS712 is shown in
Figure 3-16.

147

Figure 3-16. *ACS712 breakout board*

The breakout board shown in Figure 3-16 works with 5 V. The output of this sensor is half of the input voltage, that is, 2.5 V, when the input current is 0 A. Therefore, if you connect the output of the sensor to an analog pin of Arduino, something around 511–512 must be read.

The sensitivity and operating range of different models of ACS712 are shown in Table 3-1. For instance, when +1 A is passed through ACS712 ELC-30, its output changes to 2.5 + 0.066 = 2.566 V, and when –2 A is passed, the output voltage will be 2.5 – 2 × 0.066 = 2.368 V.

Table 3-1. *Characteristics of different types of ACS712*

ACS712 Model	Operating Range	Sensitivity
ACS712 ELC-05	± 5 A	185 mV/A
ACS712 ELC-20	± 20 A	100 mV/A
ACS712 ELC-30	± 30 A	66 mV/A

Let's make a DC ammeter with this sensor. Upload the following code to the board. This code measures the current 50 times and displays the average of measured values. Use the Serial Monitor to see the output of this code.

```
int value=0;
float Vref=5.0;
float sensorSensitivity=66e-3; //ACS712ELC-30 is used here.
float current=0;
float sum=0;
int n=50;

void setup() {
  // put your setup code here, to run once:
  Serial.begin(9600);
}

void loop() {
  // put your main code here, to run repeatedly:
  for (int i=0;i<n;i++){
    value=analogRead(A0)-511;
    sum=sum+(value*Vref/1023)/sensorSensitivity;
    delay(3);
  }

  current=sum/n;
  sum=0;
  Serial.println((String)"Measured current is: "+current);
  Serial.println("---");
  delay(500);
}
```

The hardware of this example is shown in Figure 3-17.

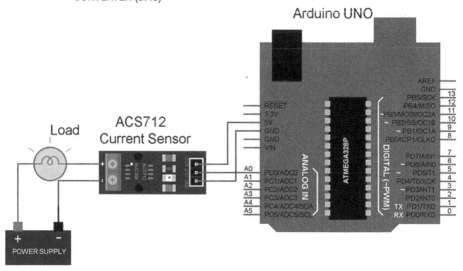

Figure 3-17. *Hardware of the studied example*

3.10 External ADC and DAC

The PCF8591 is a single-chip, single-supply low-power 8-bit CMOS data
acquisition device with four analog inputs, one analog output, and a serial
I2C-bus interface. In other words, PCF8591 can be used as an external
ADC and DAC. PCF8591 requires 90 µs to do the conversion. The breakout
board for PCF8591 is shown in Figure 3-18. Pins of the breakout board are
shown in Figure 3-19.

Figure 3-18. *PCF8591 breakout board*

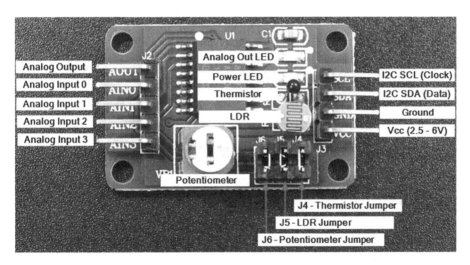

Figure 3-19. *Description of the PCF8591 breakout board's pins*

151

The schematic of the breakout board is shown in Figure 3-20.

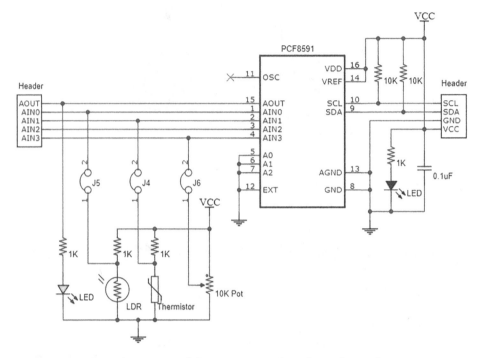

Figure 3-20. *Schematic of the PCF8591 breakout board*

3.11 PCF8591 As ADC

The following code shows how to use PCF8591 as an ADC. Upload the
code to the Arduino board:

```
/*PCF8591 Module Analog to Digital test program.
Essentially, this tests the I2C communications to the chip.
The chip address is 0x90.
*/
#include <Wire.h>
#define PCF8591 (0x90 >> 1)        // Device address = 0
```

```
#define PCF8591_DAC_ENABLE 0x40

#define PCF8591_ADC_CH0 0x40

#define PCF8591_ADC_CH1 0x41

#define PCF8591_ADC_CH2 0x42

#define PCF8591_ADC_CH3 0x43

byte adc_value;

float voltage=0;

byte getADC(byte config){
  Wire.beginTransmission(PCF8591);
  Wire.write(config);
  Wire.endTransmission();
  Wire.requestFrom((int) PCF8591,2);
  while (Wire.available()){
    adc_value = Wire.read(); //This needs two reads to get
                                the value.
    adc_value = Wire.read();
  }
  return adc_value;
 }

void setup(){
  Serial.begin(9600);
  Wire.begin();
  Serial.println("ADC Test");
}

void loop()
{
  adc_value = getADC(PCF8591_ADC_CH3); //Channel 3 is the pot
  voltage=adc_value*5.0/255.0;
```

```
Serial.println((String)"Voltage of center terminal of the
potentiometer is: "+voltage+" V.");
delay(500);
}
```

The hardware of this example is shown in Figure 3-21. Open the Serial
Monitor and rotate the potentiometer on the breakout board. The voltage
of the center terminal of the potentiometer appears on the screen.

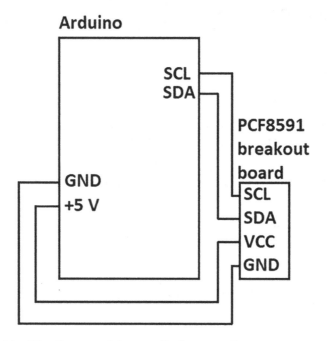

Figure 3-21. *Hardware of the studied example*

3.12 PCF8591 As DAC

The following code shows how to convert a digital data into an analog
voltage:

```
/*PCF8591 Module Digital To analog test program.
Essentially, this tests the I2C communications to the chip.
The chip address is 0x90.
*/

#include <Wire.h>
#define PCF8591 (0x90 >> 1)      // Device address = 0
#define PCF8591_DAC_ENABLE 0x40
#define PCF8591_ADC_CH0 0x40
#define PCF8591_ADC_CH1 0x41
#define PCF8591_ADC_CH2 0x42
#define PCF8591_ADC_CH3 0x43
byte dac_value=0;
byte enteredValue=0;

void putDAC(byte dac_value){
   Wire.beginTransmission(PCF8591);     //Calls the 8591 to
                                          attention.
   Wire.write(PCF8591_DAC_ENABLE);     //Send a DAC enable word.
   Wire.write(dac_value);              //Send the desired DAC
                                        value (0-255)
   Wire.endTransmission();
}

void setup(){
   Serial.begin(9600);
   Serial.println("Please enter a number in the 0-255 range:");
   Wire.begin();
}
```

```
void loop(){
    while(Serial.available()>0){
     enteredValue=Serial.parseInt();
     Serial.println((String)"Entered number is:"+enteredValue);
     putDAC(enteredValue);
     Serial.println();
     Serial.println("Please enter a number in the 0-255 range:");
    }
}
```

The hardware of this example is shown in Figure 3-22. After uploading the code to the Arduino board, open the Serial Monitor and enter a number between 0 and 255 (Figure 3-23). The digital multimeter (DMM) connected to the Aout pin shows the output voltage associated with the entered value.

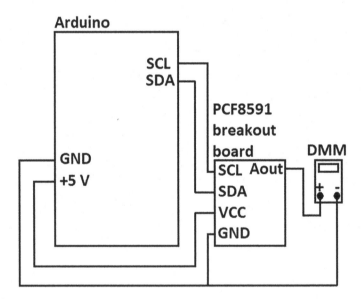

Figure 3-22. *Hardware of the studied example*

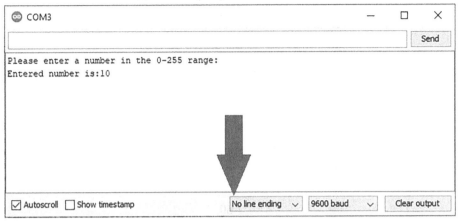

Figure 3-23. *Sample output*

Table 3-2 shows some of the entered values and voltages associated with them.

Table 3-2. *Entered values and voltages of the Aout pin*

Entered Value	Generated Voltage
0	0.024
10	0.196
20	0.388
30	0.528
40	0.728
50	0.880
60	1.06
70	1.26
80	1.46

(*continued*)

Table 3-2. (*continued*)

Entered Value	Generated Voltage
90	1.66
100	1.84
110	2.04
120	2.24
130	2.44
140	2.60
150	2.80
160	3.00
170	3.20
180	3.36
190	3.56
200	3.76
210	3.92
220	4.16
230	4.16
240	4.16
250	4.16

Figure 3-24 shows the graph of data in Table 3-2. For values bigger than 215, saturations are observed. The graph is linear for the [0, 215] region. Using curve fitting, we obtain Vout=0.01887×n−0.02726 or n=(Vout+0.02726)/0.01887 for the linear region of the graph (0≤n≤215).

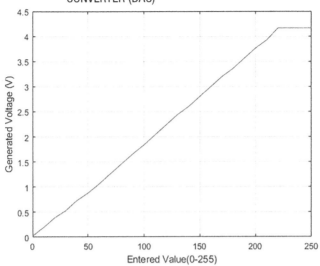

Figure 3-24. *Input-output characteristic for the PCF8591*
breakout board

3.13 References for Further Study

[1] Arduino negative voltmeter:

https://bit.ly/3FV5oP4

[2] Current measurement with ACS712:

https://bit.ly/3FSFD1D

https://bit.ly/2I8clQc

[3] PCF8591 datasheet:

https://bit.ly/3GgWZqv

[4] PCF8591:

https://bit.ly/3PXWHrU

https://bit.ly/3hXoJXF

159

CHAPTER 4

LCD and EEPROM

4.1 Introduction

In this chapter, you will learn how to connect a Liquid Crystal Display (LCD) and Electrically Erasable Programmable Read-Only Memory (EEPROM to an Arduino board. Connecting an LCD to an Arduino board permits you to make portable devices which don't require to be connected to a computer in order to show the outputs.

EEPROM plays the role of a hard disk for microcontroller systems. They can store data even when the power is turned off. ATmega328 (the microcontroller used in Arduino UNO, Nano, and Mini) has 1024 bytes of EEPROM memory. The internal EEPROM memory has a specified life of 100,000 write/erase cycles, so you may need to be careful about how often you write to it. An EEPROM write takes around 3.3 ms to complete; therefore, it is not a high-speed memory. This chapter studies both internal EEPROM and connecting an external EEPROM to Arduino boards.

Let's take a closer look at LCDs. Normally, LCDs are output devices, that is, show data to the user. However, they can be input devices as well, that is, take data from the user. For instance, touchscreen LCDs are both an output and input device. In this chapter, we will study nontouchable (i.e., character LCD) LCDs only.

© Farzin Asadi 2023
F. Asadi, *Essentials of Arduino™ Boards Programming*, Maker Innovations Series,
https://doi.org/10.1007/978-1-4842-9600-4_4

Character (or text) LCDs can be divided into two groups: parallel LCDs and I2C LCDs. Parallel LCDs have 16 pins, and they use parallel data transfer. Therefore, they eat many of the pins of your microcontroller. They require at least eight pins to work: VCC, GND, and six data pins. Therefore, they eat six digital I/O pins of your microcontroller. I2C requires only four pins: VCC, GND, and I2C pins (SCL and SDA). They don't eat digital I/O pins of your microcontroller. In the Arduino UNO board, SDA and SCL are connected to A4 and A5 pins. If you connect an I2C LCD to the board, then you cannot use A4 and A5 for analog-to-digital conversion purposes. In other words, you will lose two analog pins.

Character LCDs are known by the number of rows and number of characters that can be shown in each row. For instance, a 2×16 LCD has two rows, and each row can contain up to 16 characters.

Figure 4-1 shows a parallel LCD. Table 4-1 studies each pin in detail.

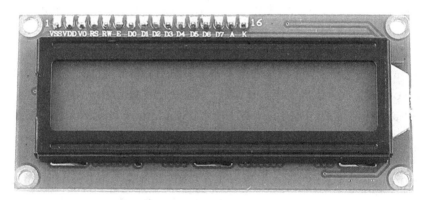

Figure 4-1. *Parallel LCD*

Chapter 4. Layout

Table 4-1. Pins of the parallel LCD

Pin No.	Pin Description	Pin Connection
Pin 1 (VSS)	This is the ground pin of the LCD	Connected to the ground of the Arduino board
Pin 2 (VDD)	This is the supply voltage of the LCD	Connected to +5 V of the Arduino board
Pin 3 (V0)	Adjusts the contrast of the LCD	Connected to a variable POT that can source 0–5 V (Figure 4-2)
Pin 4 (RS)	Toggles between command and data registers	Connected to an MCU pin and gets either 0 or 1. 0 for command mode and 1 for data mode
Pin 5 (RW)	Toggles the LCD between read and write operations	Connected to the ground
Pin 6 (E)	Enable	Connected to the Arduino board and always held high
Pin (7–14) D0...D7	Data bits	In 4-wire mode, only 4 pins (0–3) are connected to the Arduino board. In 8-wire mode, all 8 pins (0–7) are connected to the Arduino board
Pin 15 (A)	Anode of a backlight LED	Connected to +5 V through a 220 Ω resistor (Figure 4-3)
Pin 16 (K)	Cathode of a backlight LED	Connected to the ground (Figure 4-3)

Pin V0 controls the contrast of the LCD. Pin V0 needs to be connected to the center pin of a 10 kΩ potentiometer as shown in Figure 4-2. You can obtain the best quality for the text shown by the LCD using the potentiometer shown in Figure 4-2.

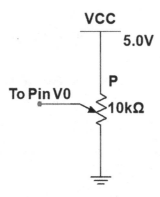

Figure 4-2. *Control of LCD contrast*

The character LCDs generally have a backlight LED which is very useful if the environment around the LCD is dark. You can turn on and off the backlight LED using the circuit shown in Figure 4-3. If your LCD has 14 pins, then it has no backlight LED.

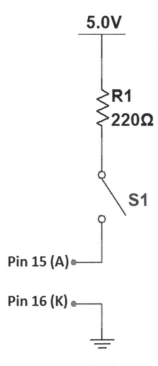

Figure 4-3. *Control of the LCD backlight*

4.2 Showing Text on Parallel LCD

This section shows how a parallel LCD can be connected to Arduino. A parallel LCD requires six pins of your Arduino board. Upload the following code to the Arduino board. After uploading the code, the number of seconds passed will be shown on the LCD screen. Connections between the Arduino board and LCD are shown as comments in the first few lines of the code.

165

After uploading the code and in the first run, the LCD may show meaningless symbols. In this case, simply press the reset button on the Arduino board to reset the system.

```
#include <LiquidCrystal.h>
/*
- LCD's VSS -> Ground pin of Arduino
- LCD's VDD -> +5 V pin of Arduino
- LCD's V0 pin -> Center terminal of potentiometer
- LCD's RS pin -> Arduino's pin 12
- LCD's R/W pin-> Ground
- LCD's Enable (E) pin -> Arduino's pin 11
- LCD's D0, D1, D2 and D3 pins -> Not connected
- LCD's D4 pin -> Arduino's pin 5
- LCD's D5 pin -> Arduino's pin 4
- LCD's D6 pin -> Arduino's pin 3
- LCD's D7 pin -> Arduino's pin 2
*/
LiquidCrystal lcd(12, 11, 5, 4, 3, 2);

void setup() {
  lcd.begin(16, 2); //number of column and rows
  lcd.print("Time elpassed:");
}
void loop() {
  lcd.setCursor(0,1); // cursor is put at first column of
                          second row
  lcd.print((String)(millis()/1000)+" sec.");
}
```

4.3 Showing Text on I2C Serial LCD

A parallel LCD eats six pins of your Arduino board. Serial LCDs use an I2C protocol to transfer data and require only two pins. Upload the following code to the Arduino board. Connections between the Arduino board and LCD are shown as comments in the first few lines of the code.

After uploading the code and in the first run, the LCD may show meaningless symbols. In this case, simply press the reset button on the Arduino board to reset the system.

```
// Connect SCL pin of LCD to SCL pin of Arduino
// Connect SDA pin of LCD to SDA pin of Arduino
// Connect the VCC pin of LCD to +5 V of Arduino
// Connect the GND pin of LCD to ground of Arduino

int Address=0x27;

#include <Wire.h>
#include <LiquidCrystal_I2C.h> //https://www.arduino.cc/
reference/en/libraries/liquidcrystal-i2c/

LiquidCrystal_I2C lcd(Address, 16, 2);
int i=0;

void setup() {
  // put your setup code here, to run once:
  lcd.init();
  lcd.backlight(); //Turns on the backlight
  //lcd.noBacklight(); //Turns off the backlight
}

void loop() {
  // put your main code here, to run repeatedly:
  lcd.setCursor(0,0); // (Column, Row)
  i=i+1;
```

```
lcd.print((String)"i= "+i);
delay(1000);

lcd.setCursor(0,1);
lcd.print("Second Line...");
}
```

If the preceding code doesn't work

1) Open the Arduino IDE and upload the File ➤ Examples ➤ Wire ➤ I2C_Scanner code to the Arduino board in order to find the correct address of the serial LCD.

2) After uploading the I2C_Scanner, open Tools ➤ Serial Monitor to see the correct address of the serial LCD.

3) Update the address line of the preceding code, that is, int Address=0x27;, based on the correct address and upload the correct code to the Arduino. This time, the code must work.

4.4 Internal EEPROM

The following code writes a random number between 0 and 255 to the location 0 of EEPROM and reads the content of location 0.

The following code uses the EEPROM.update(address, value) command to write a value at the location determined by the address. You can use the EEPROM.write(address, value) command to write a value at the location determined by the address as well. However, the use of the EEPROM.update command is recommended. Because the EEPROM. update command compares the value that is requested to be written with the current content of that location. If two values are the same, then no writing takes place. However, the EEPROM.write command writes the value even when the two values (the value requested to be written and the current content of that address) are the same. Remember that the number of writings to EEPROM is limited. Therefore, EEPROM.update doesn't consume the lifetime of the EEPROM without reason.

```
#include <EEPROM.h>
byte a=0;
int selection=0;

void setup()
{
  Serial.begin(9600);
  randomSeed(analogRead(A0));
  Serial.println("1.Write to EEPROM");
  Serial.println("2.Read EEPROM");
}

void loop(){
  if (Serial.available()>0){
    selection=Serial.parseInt();

    if (selection==1){
      a=random(255+1); //value of generated random number a is
                        between 0 and 255.
      EEPROM.update(0,a);
      Serial.println((String)"\n"+a+" is written to the
      EEPROM...");
    }

    if (selection==2){
      Serial.println((String)"Value of EEPROM at location 0 is:
      "+EEPROM.read(0)+".\n");
    }
  }
}
```

Note that in EEPROM.write and EEPROM.update functions, the value that is requested to be stored in the EEPROM must be an integer between 0 and 255. If you try to save a value n that is equal or bigger than 256, then $n - 256 * \left\lfloor \dfrac{n}{256} \right\rfloor$ is stored in the requested location. For instance, EEPROM. write(0,6666); writes 10 to location 0 of EEPROM. As another example, EEPROM.write(0,6.73); writes 6 to location 0 of EEPROM.

4.5 get() and put() Commands

With the aid of EEPROM.put() and EEPROM.get() functions, you can put and read any data type to the EEPROM memory. The following code puts three double numbers in the EEPROM memory and reads them:

```
#include <EEPROM.h>
double a=1.23;
double b=45.67;
double c=890.12;
double readValue=0.00;

int selection=0;
int n=0;

void setup() {
  // put your setup code here, to run once:
  Serial.begin(9600);

  Serial.println("Note that: a=1.23, b=45.67, c=890.12");
  Serial.println();
  Serial.println("Enter your command (1,2,3).1, reads a, 2
  reads b and 3 reads c.");
  Serial.println();
```

```
  EEPROM.put(0,a);
  EEPROM.put(sizeof(a),b);
  EEPROM.put(sizeof(a)+sizeof(b),c);
}

void loop() {
  // put your main code here, to run repeatedly:
  if (Serial.available()>0){
    selection=Serial.parseInt();

    if (selection==1){
      n=0;
      EEPROM.get(n,readValue);
      Serial.println((String)"Value stored at location 0 is:
      "+readValue+".");
    };

    if (selection==2){
      n=sizeof(a);
      EEPROM.get(n,readValue);
      Serial.println((String)"Value stored at location "+n+"
      is: "+readValue+".");
    };

    if (selection==3){
      n=sizeof(a)+sizeof(b);
      EEPROM.get(n,readValue);
      Serial.println((String)"Value stored at location "+n+"
      is: "+readValue+".");
    };
  }
}
```

4.6 External EEPROM

External EEPROM ICs can be used to store what you want. In this section, we will see how 24LC16B EEPROM can be connected to Arduino. The WP (Write Protect) pin of 24LC16B must be connected to 0 V; otherwise, you cannot write over it. Upload the following code to the Arduino. This code writes and retrieves the byte data type:

```
//Download the library from https://www.arduino.cc/reference/
en/libraries/i2c_eeprom/
// See: https://github.com/RobTillaart/I2C_EEPROM

#include "Wire.h"
#include "I2C_eeprom.h"
byte x[]={0,1,2,3,4};
byte y[]={10,1,2,3,40};
byte z[]={0,0,0,0,0,0};

I2C_eeprom ee(0x50, I2C_DEVICESIZE_24LC16);

void setup() {
  // put your setup code here, to run once:
  Serial.begin(9600);
  ee.begin();
}

void loop() {
  // put your main code here, to run repeatedly:
  ee.writeBlock(0, (uint8_t *) &x, sizeof(x)); // Starts from
                                               location 0 and
                                               writes array x
  ee.writeByte(5,7); //Writes 7 at location 5
  for (int i=0;i<6;i++){
```

```
    Serial.println((String)"At location "+i+" of EEPROM "+ee.
    readByte(i)+" is written.");
  }

  Serial.println();
  ee.updateBlock(0, (uint8_t *) &y, sizeof(y));
  for (int i=0;i<6;i++){
    Serial.println((String)"At location "+i+" of EEPROM "+ee.
    readByte(i)+" is written.");
  }

  Serial.println();
  ee.readBlock(0, (uint8_t *) &z, 6);
  for (int i=0;i<6;i++){
    Serial.println((String)"z("+i+")= "+z[i]+" is written.");
  }

  Serial.println();
  ee.setBlock(0,1, 6); //Writes 1 in the first 6 locations
  for (int i=0;i<6;i++){
    Serial.println((String)"At location "+i+" of EEPROM "+ee.
    readByte(i)+" is written.");
  }

  delay(60000);
}
```

The hardware of this example is shown in Figure 4-4. Open the Serial Monitor and see the output.

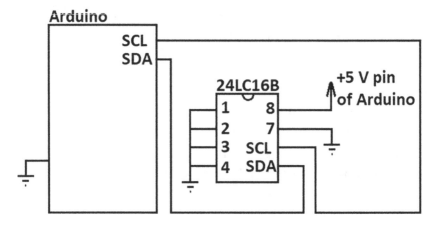

Figure 4-4. *Hardware of the studied example*

4.7 Writing and Reading Integer Numbers to the External EEPROM

The following example shows how an integer data type can be written to and read from an external EEPROM:

```
#include "Wire.h"
#include "I2C_eeprom.h"

float x=12.34;
float y=0;

I2C_eeprom ee(0x50, I2C_DEVICESIZE_24LC16);

void setup() {
  // put your setup code here, to run once:
  Serial.begin(9600);
  ee.begin();
  ee.setBlock(0,0,sizeof(x));
  ee.writeBlock(0,(uint8_t *) &x, sizeof(x));
}
```

```
void loop() {
  // put your main code here, to run repeatedly:
  ee.readBlock(0,(uint8_t *) &y, sizeof(y));
  Serial.println(y);
  delay(10000);
}
```

The hardware of this example is shown in Figure 4-5. Use the Serial Monitor to see the output of this code.

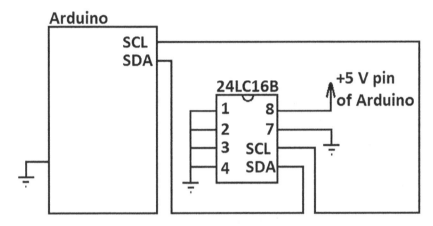

Figure 4-5. *Hardware of the studied example*

4.8 Writing and Reading Structures to the External EEPROM

The following example shows how structures can be written to and read from an external EEPROM:

```
#include "Wire.h"
#include "I2C_eeprom.h"

I2C_eeprom ee(0x50, I2C_DEVICESIZE_24LC16);
```

```
struct measurement{
  float temp;
  int pressure;
  char* location;
};

void setup() {
  // put your setup code here, to run once:
  Serial.begin(9600);
  ee.begin();
  ee.setBlock(0,0,sizeof(measurement));
}

void loop() {
  // put your main code here, to run repeatedly:
  measurement m1;
  measurement m2;

  m1.temp=32.7;
  m1.pressure=12;
  m1.location="Inside the city.";

  ee.writeBlock(0, (uint8_t *) &m1, sizeof(m1));
  ee.readBlock(0, (uint8_t *) &m2, sizeof(m2));

  Serial.println((String)"m2.temp="+m2.temp);
  Serial.println((String)"m2.pressure="+m2.pressure);
  Serial.println((String)"m2.location="+m2.location);
  Serial.println("-----");
  delay(10000);
}
```

The hardware of this example is shown in Figure 4-6. Use the Serial Monitor to see the output of this code.

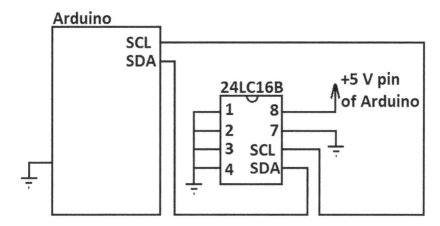

Figure 4-6. *Hardware of the studied example*

4.9 References for Further Study

[1]   LiquidCrystal I2C library:

https://bit.ly/3FXIGWf

[2]   24LC16B datasheet:

https://bit.ly/3G2I7uG

[3]   Connection of external EEPROM to the Arduino:

https://bit.ly/3WJBqnT

https://bit.ly/3Vo1Bzu

[4]   EEPROM library:

https://bit.ly/3VkR3Rr

[5]   I2C_EEPROM library:

https://bit.ly/3WrA55d

https://bit.ly/3WLRZiS

177

CHAPTER 5

Serial Communication

5.1 Introduction

This chapter focuses on universal asynchronous receiver/transmitter (UART)–based serial communication between the Arduino board and your computer. Serial communication uses pins 0 and 1 (Figure 5-1). Serial communication helps us to show results on the computer screen with the aid of a tool called Serial Monitor. A Serial Monitor is a part of the Arduino IDE. For instance, assume that you read the voltage of an analog pin. In this case, you have two options to see the measured value: (1) use an LCD and show the measured value on it; (2) use serial communication and show the measured value on a computer screen. The first method requires an LCD, and the LCD must be connected to the Arduino board using suitable connections. However, in the second method, everything is prepared already, and you need to write a few lines of code. In the second method, data transfer will be done using the USB cable connected between the computer and the Arduino board.

© Farzin Asadi 2023
F. Asadi, *Essentials of Arduino™ Boards Programming*, Maker Innovations Series,
https://doi.org/10.1007/978-1-4842-9600-4_5

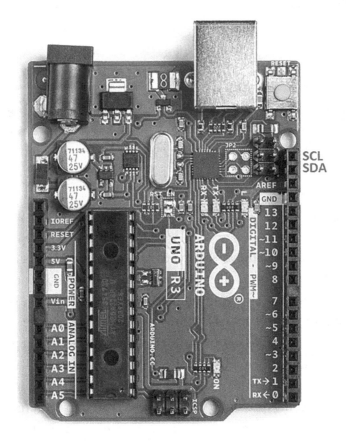

Figure 5-1. *Arduino UNO board*

A UART channel has two data lines. There is an RX pin and a TX pin on each device (RX for receive and TX for transmit). Each device's RX pin is connected to the other device's TX pin (Figure 5-2). Note that there are no shared clock lines! This is the asynchronous aspect of the universal asynchronous receiver/transmitter.

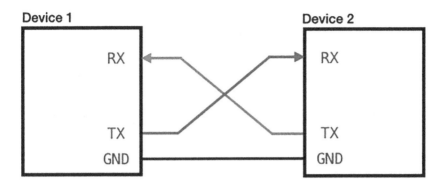

Figure 5-2. *Serial communication*

As a kind of asynchronous serial communication protocol, UART works by transmitting each binary bit of the transmitted data bit by bit.

Serial communication refers to the use of a transmission line to sequentially transmit data bit by bit, or two signal lines can be used to form full-duplex communication, such as RS232. The characteristic is that the communication line is simple, the communication can be realized by using a simple cable, the cost is reduced, and it is suitable for the application of long-distance communication, but the transmission speed is slow.

The data transfer rate is expressed in the baud rate, that is, the number of bits transmitted per second. For example, if the data transmission rate is 120 characters/second, and each character is 10 bits (1 start bit, 7 data bits, 1 check bit, 1 stop bit), then the baud rate of its transmission is 10×120 = 1200 bits/second = 1200 baud. Refer to [1] if you are not familiar with UART-based serial communication.

The Serial Monitor (Figure 5-3) is a tool to receive/send data from/ to the Arduino board connected to the computer. Use the baud section in Figure 5-3 to set the baud rate. Baud rates supported by the Serial Monitor are shown in Figure 5-4.

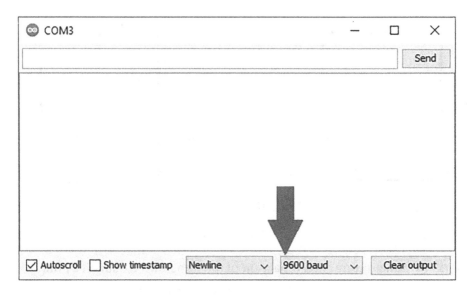

Figure 5-3. *Serial Monitor window*

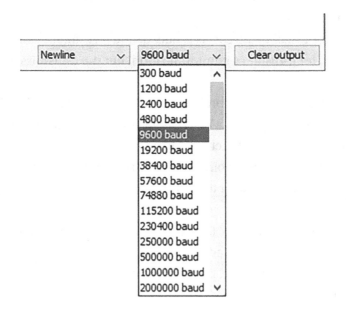

Figure 5-4. *Supported baud rates*

You need to click Tools ➤ Serial Monitor (Figure 5-5) in order to run the Serial Monitor program.

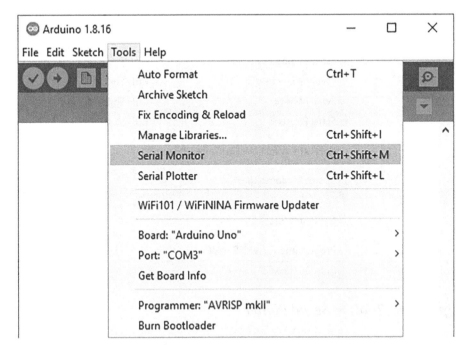

Figure 5-5. *Tools ➤ Serial Monitor*

The Serial Plotter (Figure 5-6) is another useful software that is available in the Arduino IDE. It shows the data graphically (see Section 3.4).

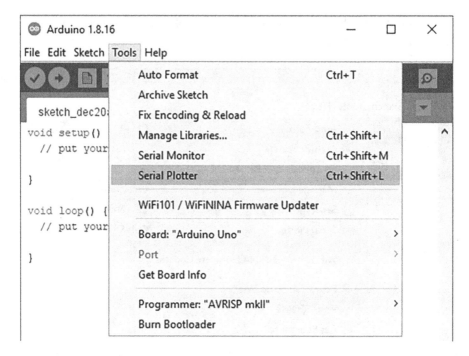

Figure 5-6. *Tools ➤ Serial Plotter*

5.2 Observing the Data Transfer with an Oscilloscope

In this section, we will use an oscilloscope to observe the data transfer between the Arduino board and the computer. Let's start. Upload the following code to the Arduino board. This code continuously sends data to the computer. Arduino is the sender, and the computer is the receiver.

```
int a=10;

void setup() {
  // put your setup code here, to run once:
  Serial.begin(9600);
}
```

```
void loop() {
  // put your main code here, to run repeatedly:
  Serial.println(a);
}
```

After uploading the code to the board, connect an oscilloscope to pin 1. Now you can see the data that is sent to the computer from Arduino. You can open the Serial Monitor and see the data that comes from the Arduino as well.

Now upload the following code to the Arduino board. This code receives the data that comes from the computer. Arduino is the receiver in this example, and the computer is the sender.

```
int a=0;

void setup() {
  // put your setup code here, to run once:
  Serial.begin(9600);
}

void loop() {
  // put your main code here, to run repeatedly:
  if (Serial.available()>0)
    a=Serial.parseInt();
}
```

Connect an oscilloscope to pin 0. Open the Serial Monitor and enter a number to the box shown in Figure 5-7. Then press the Enter key. When you press the Enter key, you will see some pulses on the oscilloscope screen. This is the data that comes from the computer toward the Arduino board.

Figure 5-7. *Sending a number to the Arduino board*

5.3 Sending a String to a Computer

In this example, we want to send a string from the Arduino board to the computer. Upload the following code to the board. The Serial.println command is used to transfer the data from Arduino to the computer.

```
long randNumber=0;

void setup() {
  // put your setup code here, to run once:
  Serial.begin(9600);
  randomSeed(analogRead(0));
}

void loop() {
  // put your main code here, to run repeatedly:
```

```
randNumber=random(101); //generates a random number from
0 to 100
Serial.println((String)"generated random number is:
"+randNumber+".");
delay(500);
}
```

After uploading the code, open the Serial Monitor in order to see the output of the code.

5.4 Receiving a String from a Computer

In this example, the Arduino board receives a string from the computer with the aid of Serial.available and Serial.readString commands. This code turns on the onboard LED when the entered string is "on," "ON," or "On." The onboard LED will be turned off when the entered string is "off," "OFF," or "Off." The onboard LED keeps the previous state for other entered strings.

```
//https://www.arduino.cc/reference/en/language/functions/
communication/serial/readstring/

void setup() {
  // put your setup code here, to run once:
  Serial.begin(9600);
  pinMode(LED_BUILTIN,OUTPUT);
}

void loop() {
  if (Serial.available()>0){
    String inputCommand=Serial.readString();
    Serial.println((String)"Entered command: "+inputCommand);

    if (inputCommand=="on" ||inputCommand=="ON"||inputCommand==
    "On")
    {
```

```
    digitalWrite(LED_BUILTIN,HIGH);
  }

  if (inputCommand=="off"||inputCommand=="OFF"||inputCommand==
  "Off")
  {
    digitalWrite(LED_BUILTIN,LOW);
  }

  }
}
```

Open the Serial Monitor after uploading the code to the board. Enter the command into the Serial Monitor window and press the Enter key to run it (Figure 5-8). Select the "No line ending" to avoid addition of anything to what you entered.

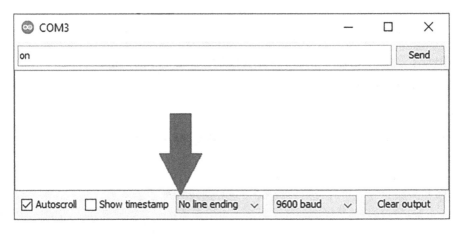

Figure 5-8. *Sending a command string to the Arduino board*

5.5 Receiving Floating-Point Numbers

In this example, the Arduino board receives a floating-point number from the computer with the aid of Serial.available and Serial.parseFloat commands. This code considers the entered floating-point number as a radius of a circle and calculates the area for the given radius:

```
//https://www.arduino.cc/reference/en/language/functions/
communication/serial/parsefloat/
//parsInt command exist as well.

float radius=0;
float area=0;

void setup() {
  // put your setup code here, to run once:
  Serial.begin(9600);
  Serial.println("Strated...");
}

void loop() {

  if (Serial.available()>0){
    radius=Serial.parseFloat();
    area=PI*pow(radius,2);

    Serial.println((String)"Entered radius: "+radius+"
    Area= "+area);
    Serial.println();
  }
}
```

Open the Serial Monitor after uploading the code to the board. Enter the radius into the Serial Monitor window and press the Enter key to see the calculated area (Figure 5-9). Select the "No line ending" to avoid addition of anything to what you entered.

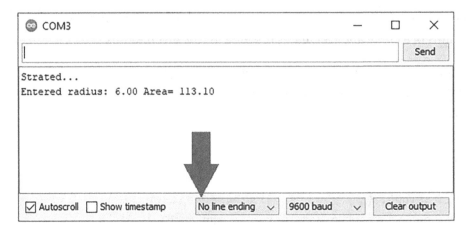

Figure 5-9. *Sample output of the code*

5.6 Receiving Integer Numbers

In this example, the Arduino board receives an integer number from the computer with the aid of Serial.available and Serial.parseInt commands. Then the code prints the first n terms of the Fibonacci series, where n shows the integer number entered by the user:

```
int incomingNumber=0;
int a=1;
int b=1;
int c=0;
int s=0;
void setup() {
  // put your setup code here, to run once:
  Serial.begin(9600);
  Serial.println("Enter the number of terms that you want.");
}
```

```
void loop() {
  // put your main code here, to run repeatedly:
  if (Serial.available()>0){
    incomingNumber=Serial.parseInt();
    Serial.println((String)"User entered "+incomingNumber+".");
  Serial.print("1,1,");
  for (int i=1;i<=incomingNumber-2;i++){
   s=a+b;
   Serial.print((String)s+',');
   c=a;
   a=b;
   b=c+b;
  }
  }
}
```

Open the Serial Monitor after uploading the code to the board. Enter the number of terms that you want into the Serial Monitor window and press the Enter key to see the output (Figure 5-10). Select the "No line ending" to avoid addition of anything to what you entered.

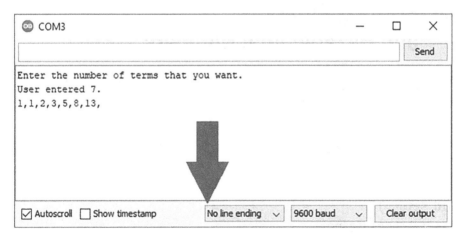

Figure 5-10. *Sample output of the code*

5.7 Printing the Quotation Mark

The quotation mark must be written as \" inside the Serial.print and Serial.println commands. The following is an example:

```
void setup() {
  // put your setup code here, to run once:
  Serial.begin(9600);
}

void loop() {
  // put your main code here, to run repeatedly:
  Serial.println("\"Hello World!\" is the first program that
  programmers write.");
  Serial.println("'Hello World!\' is the first program that
  programmers write.");
  Serial.println();
  delay(120000);
}
```

5.8 Printing Binary and Hexadecimal Numbers

Serial.print and Serial.println commands can print the binary and hexadecimal representations of a variable. The following is an example. Note that 45 in decimal is equal to 00101101 in binary and 2D in hexadecimal.

```
byte b = 45;

void setup() {
  Serial.begin(9600);
  Serial.println(b);        // print in decimal by default
```

```
    Serial.println(b, DEC); // print in decimal, same as above
    Serial.println(b, BIN); // print in binary
    Serial.println(b, HEX); // print in hexadecimal
}
void loop() {
}
```

Open the Serial Monitor after uploading the code to the board. The output of the code is shown in the Serial Monitor window.

5.9 Useful Functions for String Variables

The following code introduces some of the most important functions for String variables:

```
String str="ABC DEF";
String str2="ABC DEF";
String str3="xyz";
String str4="ABC dEf";
int n=0;

void setup(){
    // put your setup code here, to run once:
    Serial.begin(9600);
}

void loop(){
    // put your main code here, to run repeatedly:
    Serial.println((String)"Given string is: "+str);
    Serial.println();

    Serial.println((String)"length of this string is:
    "+str.length());
```

```
for (int i=0;i<str.length();i++)
  Serial.println((String)"charAt("+i+") is:"+str.charAt(i));

Serial.println();
Serial.println((String)"\"ABC DEF\" is compared with
\"ABC DEF\" (comparison is case sensitive). Result is:
"+str.equals(str2));
Serial.println((String)"\"ABC DEF\" is compared with
\"xyz\" (comparison is case sensitive). Result is:
"+str.equals(str4));
Serial.println((String)"\"ABC DEF\" is compared with
\"ABC dEf\" (comparison is not case sensitive). Result is:
"+str.equalsIgnoreCase(str3));

Serial.println();
str.toLowerCase();  //Result is saved in the str variable.
Serial.println("Conversion of \"ABC DEF\" to lower case: "+str);
str3.toUpperCase(); //Result is saved in the str variable.
Serial.println("Conversion of \"xyz\" to upper case: "+str3);

String str5="ABC DEF     ";
str5.trim(); //trim the white space off the string
Serial.println();
Serial.println((String)"After trimming \"ABC DEF
\" is converted to:\""+str5+"\"");

String str6="Hello World!";
Serial.println();
Serial.println("str6=\"Hello World!\"");
Serial.println((String)"Value of str6 before running the
replace command: "+str6);
str6.replace("World","Arduino");
```

```
Serial.println((String)"Value of str6 after  running the
replace command: "+str6);

Serial.println();
String str7="ABCDEFGHIJKLM";
str7.remove(2,3);
Serial.println((String)"remove(2,3) is applied to
\"ABCDEFGHIJKLM\". Result is: \""+str7+"\".");

String str8="123";
int sum1=str8.toInt()+5;
Serial.println();
Serial.println((String)"sum= "+sum1+". Expected value
is 128.");

String str9="123.456";
float sum2=str9.toFloat()+5.0;
Serial.println();
Serial.println((String)"sum= "+sum2+". Expected value is
128.456.");

String str10="123.456";
double sum3=str10.toDouble()+5.0;
Serial.println();
Serial.println((String)"sum= "+sum3+". Expected value is
128.456.");

Serial.println("-------------------------------------------");
delay(180000);
}
```

Open the Serial Monitor after uploading the code to the board. The output of the code is shown in the Serial Monitor window.

5.10 Useful Functions for Character Variables

The Arduino IDE has many useful functions to work with character variables. A list of these functions can be found in the Characters section of the Arduino website (Figure 5-11).

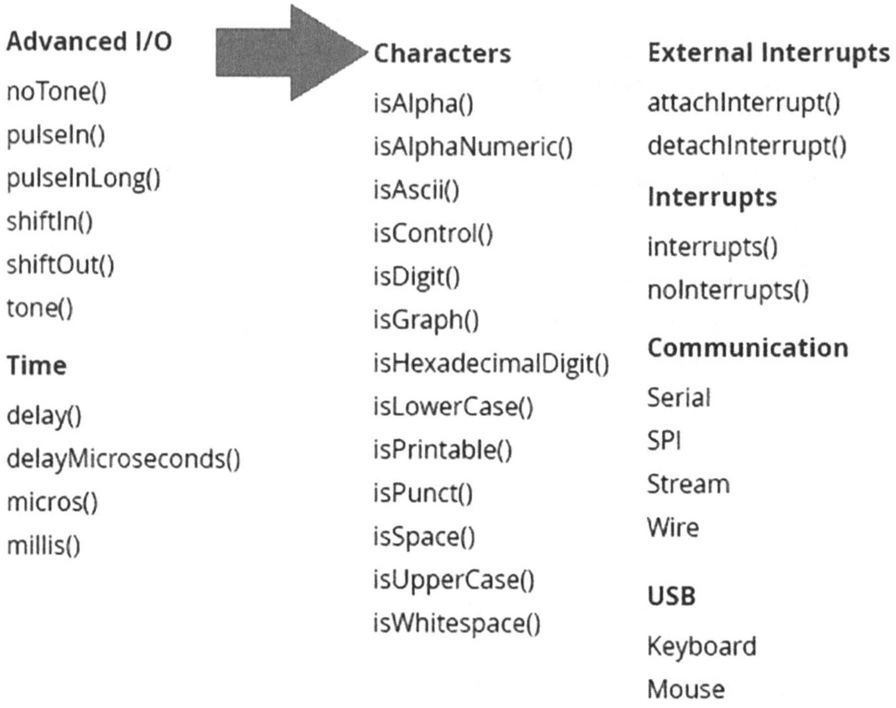

Advanced I/O

noTone()

pulseIn()

pulseInLong()

shiftIn()

shiftOut()

tone()

Time

delay()

delayMicroseconds()

micros()

millis()

Characters

isAlpha()

isAlphaNumeric()

isAscii()

isControl()

isDigit()

isGraph()

isHexadecimalDigit()

isLowerCase()

isPrintable()

isPunct()

isSpace()

isUpperCase()

isWhitespace()

External Interrupts

attachInterrupt()

detachInterrupt()

Interrupts

interrupts()

noInterrupts()

Communication

Serial

SPI

Stream

Wire

USB

Keyboard

Mouse

Figure 5-11. *Commands related to characters (see* www.arduino.cc/ *reference/en/)*

Let's study an example. The following code takes a character and checks to see whether it is lowercase, uppercase, or a number:

```
char ch1;

void setup() {
  // put your setup code here, to run once:
  Serial.begin(9600);
}

void loop() {
  // put your main code here, to run repeatedly:
  ch1=Serial.read();

  if (Serial.available()>0){
  Serial.println((String)"ch1="+ch1);

  if (isUpperCase(ch1)){
    Serial.println("variable ch1 is UPPERCASE.");
  }else{
    Serial.println("variable ch1 is lowercase.");
  }

  if (isDigit(ch1)){
    Serial.println("variable ch1 is a digit.");
  }else{
    Serial.println("variable ch1 is not a digit.");
  }

  Serial.println();
  }
  delay(1000);
}
```

Open the Serial Monitor after uploading the code to the board. The output of the code is shown in the Serial Monitor window. Sample outputs for "a" and "Ab1" are shown in Figures 5-12 and 5-13.

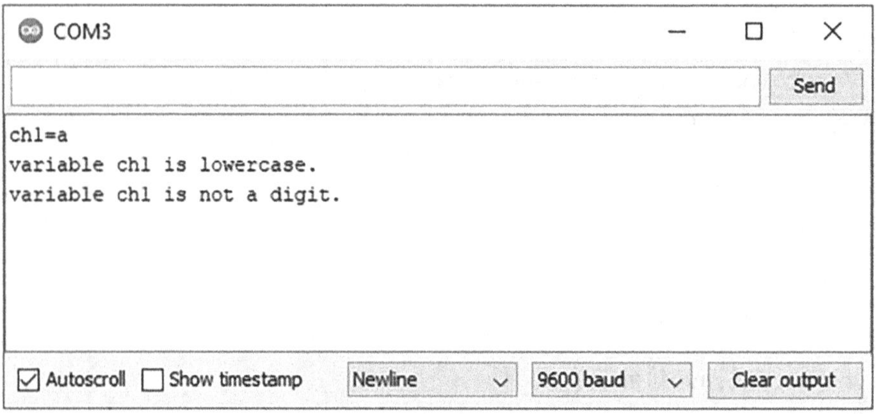

Figure 5-12. *Sample output for "a"*

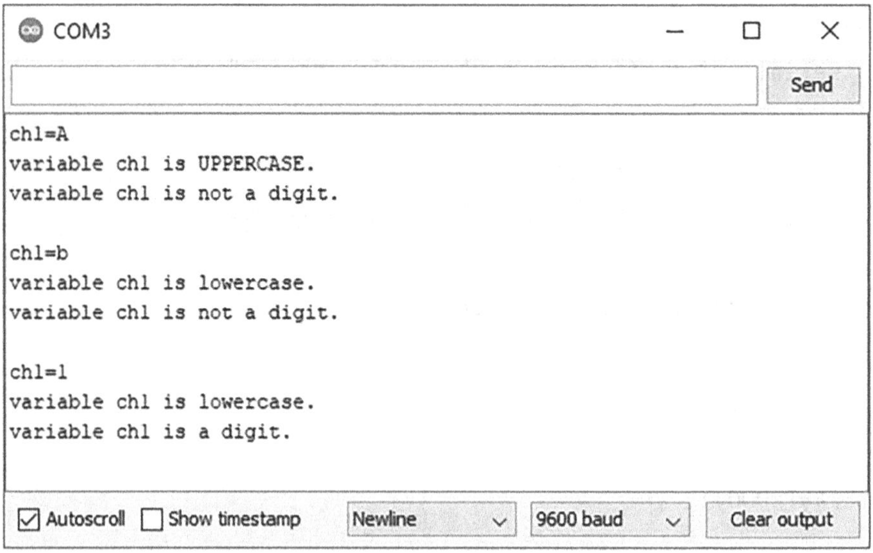

Figure 5-13. *Sample output for "Ab1"*

5.11 References for Further Study

[1]   UART communication protocol:

https://bit.ly/3WGO4X3

[2]   Comparison of UART with I2C and SPI:

https://bit.ly/3HZvyTr

[3]   String library:

https://bit.ly/2LLOzbI

CHAPTER 6

Mathematical Functions

6.1 Introduction

Mathematical operations are indispensable part of many programs. This chapter shows how mathematical operations can be done with Arduino.

6.2 Basic Mathematical Function

Most of the basic mathematical functions can be found in the following code. After uploading the code to the board, open the Serial Monitor using Tools ➤ Serial Monitor in order to see the output of the code.

```
//https://www.arduino.cc/en/math/h
//asin can be calculated with the aid of //https://
tr.wikipedia.org/wiki/Ters_trigonometrik_fonksiyonlar
void setup() {
  // put your setup code here, to run once:
  Serial.begin(9600);
  randomSeed(analogRead(0));
}
```

© Farzin Asadi 2023
F. Asadi, *Essentials of Arduino™ Boards Programming*, Maker Innovations Series,
https://doi.org/10.1007/978-1-4842-9600-4_6

```
void loop() {
    Serial.println("Compare the given results with what
    calculated by Arduino.");

    Serial.println();
    float x=12.34;
    float y=5.678;
    float z=x/y;
    int t=x/y;
    Serial.println();
    Serial.println((String) "Note that 12.34/5.678=2.17330");
    Serial.println((String) "float z=12.34/5.678= "+z);
    Serial.println((String) "int   t=12.34/5.678= "+t);

    Serial.println();
    Serial.println((String) "Reminder of 5/2 is:"+5%2);
    Serial.println((String) "Reminder of 7/4 is:"+7%4);

    Serial.println();
    Serial.println("sin, cos and tan takes the angle in
    RADYANS.");
    Serial.println((String)"Note that sin(pi/6)=0.5");
    Serial.println((String) "sin(pi/6)= "+sin(PI/6));

    Serial.println();
    Serial.println((String)"Note that cos(pi/6)=0.866");
    Serial.println((String) "cos(pi/6)= "+cos(PI/6));

    Serial.println();
    Serial.println((String)"Note that tan(pi/6)=0.5774");
    Serial.println((String) "tan(pi/6)= "+tan(PI/6));

    Serial.println();
    Serial.println((String)"Note that cot(pi/6)=1.7319");
    Serial.println((String) "cot(pi/6)= "+1/tan(PI/6));
```

```
Serial.println();
Serial.println((String)"Note that atan(1.5)=0.98279 Rad");
Serial.println((String) "atan(1.5)= "+atan(1.5));
Serial.println((String) "atan2(1.5,1)= "+atan2(1.5,1));
Serial.println((String) "atan2(-1.5,-1)= "+atan2(-1.5,-1));

Serial.println();
Serial.println((String)"Note that exp(2.6)=13.4637");
Serial.println((String) "exp(2.6)= "+exp(2.6));

Serial.println();
Serial.println((String)"Note that ln(2)=0.6931 and
log10(2)=0.3010");
Serial.println((String) "log(2)= "+log(2));
Serial.println((String) "log10(2)= "+log10(2));

Serial.println();
Serial.println((String) "floor(1.2)= "+floor(1.2));
Serial.println((String) "floor(-1.2)= "+floor(-1.2));
Serial.println((String) "ceil(1.2)= "+ceil(1.2));
Serial.println((String) "ceil(-1.2)= "+ceil(-1.2));

Serial.println((String) "abs(-123)= "+abs(-123));
Serial.println((String) "abs(-123.456)= "+abs(-123.456));

Serial.println();
Serial.println((String)"Note that 5.2^3.4=271.901");
Serial.println((String) "5.2^3.4= "+pow(5.2,3.4));

Serial.println();
Serial.println((String)"Note that 7.3^0.5=2.7019");
Serial.println((String) "sqrt(7.3)= "+sqrt(7.3));
```

```
Serial.println();
Serial.println((String) "square of 1.23, i.e. 1.23^2= "+
sq(1.23));
Serial.println((String) "square root of 1.23, i.e.
1.23^0.5= "+ sqrt(1.23));

Serial.println();
Serial.println((String) "Random number between 10 and 20:
"+random(10,20+1));
Serial.println((String) "Random number between 0 and 20:
"+random(20+1));

Serial.println();
Serial.println((String) "Max(1.23,4.56)= "+
max(1.23,4.56));
Serial.println((String) "Min(1.23,4.56)= "+
min(1.23,4.56));

Serial.println(); //https://www.arduino.cc/reference/en/
language/functions/math/constrain/
Serial.println((String) "constrain(0,1,10)=
"+constrain(0,1,10));
Serial.println((String) "constrain(5,1,10)=
"+constrain(5,1,10));
Serial.println((String) "constrain(15,1,10)=
"+constrain(15,1,10));

delay(60000);
}
```

6.3 Overflow of Variables

When you use a variable, you must ensure that the value that it saves lies in the allowed range for that variable. For instance, integer (int) variables can take a number from –32768 to +32767. If a stored value is outside of this range, then it is not stored correctly. For instance, in the following code, 33000 is assigned to an int variable:

```
//int take values from -32768 to 32767
//unsigned int take values from 0 to 65535
//short take values from -32768 to 32767
//long take values from -2147483648 to 2147483647
//unsigned long take values from 0 to 4294967295
//byte take values from 0 to 255
//word take values from 0 65535
//float take values from -3.4028235E38 to +3.4028235E38

int i=33000;

void setup() {
  // put your setup code here, to run once:
  Serial.begin(9600);
}

void loop() {
  // put your main code here, to run repeatedly:
  Serial.println("Value of 33000 is assigned to int
  variable i.");
  Serial.println((String)"Value of i is: "+i);

  delay(10000);
}
```

Upload the code to the board and open the Serial Monitor to see the output. As shown in Figure 6-1, the value of variable i is not the expected value (33000).

Figure 6-1. *Overflow of a variable*

6.4 E Notation

You can use the E or e in order to enter numbers given in scientific format. In the following code, a=1000, b=0.053, and c=0.000123. Note that the output of this code for a×c is rounded to 0.00.

```
double a=1E3;
double b=5.3E-2;
double c=1.23e-4;

void setup() {
  // put your setup code here, to run once:
  Serial.begin(9600);
}
```

```
void loop() {
  // put your main code here, to run repeatedly:
  Serial.println("1000*0.053=53");
  Serial.println((String)"a*b= "+a*b);
  Serial.println();

  Serial.println("1000*0.000123=0.123");
  Serial.println((String)"a*c= "+a*c);
  Serial.println();

  Serial.println("0.053*0.000123=0.0000065190");
  Serial.println((String)"b*c= "+b*c);
  Serial.println();

  delay(15000);
}
```

6.5 Map Function

The map function linearly converts values from an input range to values from another range. For instance, assume that we are given a value x from the $[a, b]$ interval, that is, $x \in [a, b]$. We want to find value y from $[c, d]$ that is linearly proportional with the given point and interval. We need to solve $\dfrac{x-a}{b-a} + a = \dfrac{y-a}{d-c} + c$. After simple algebraic operations, we reach to $y = \dfrac{d-c}{b-a}(x-a) + (d-c)(a-c) + c$. The map function implements this formula. For instance, int mappedVal=map(328,0,1024,0,255) converts 328 from [0,1024] into a proportional value from the [0,255] interval (x=328, a=0, b=1024, c=0, d=255). This command returns 81.

In the following code, the reading of analog pin A0 which is a value between 0 and 1023 is linearly converted to a value from the [0, 255] interval (Figure 6-2). The converted value is used as a duty cycle for PWM generation. The PWM signal controls the intensity of the LED connected to pin 9 (Figure 6-3).

```
int dutyCycle=0;

void setup() {
  pinMode(9,OUTPUT);
}

void loop() {
  dutyCycle = analogRead(A0);
  dutyCycle = map(dutyCycle, 0, 1023, 0, 255);
  analogWrite(9, dutyCycle);
}
```

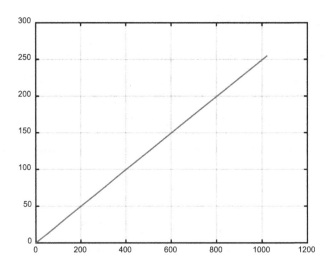

Figure 6-2. *Linear conversion of [0, 1023] to [0, 255]*

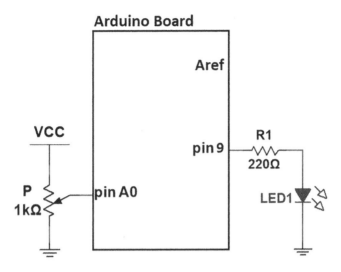

Figure 6-3. *The intensity of the LED is controlled with a potentiometer*

6.6 sizeof Operator

The sizeof operator returns the number of bytes in a variable type or the number of bytes occupied by an array. Upload the following code to the board. Use the Serial Monitor to see the output of the code. Note that for Arduino UNO, float and double data types are the same. However, in the Arduino DUE board, a float takes 4 bytes and double takes 8 bytes.

```
int a=1;            //a take values from -32768 to 32767
unsigned int b=1;   //b take values from 0 to 65535
short c=1;          //c take values from -32768 to 32767
long d=1;           //d take values from -2147483648 to
                          2147483647
unsigned long e=1;  //e take values from 0 to 4294967295
byte f=1;           //f take values from 0 to 255
word g=1;           //g take values from 0 65535
```

```
float h=1.0;          //h take values from -3.4028235E38 to
                      +3.4028235E38
double i=1.0;
char j='a';
bool k=false;
char ch[]={'A','r','d','u','i','n','o'};

void setup() {
  // put your setup code here, to run once:
  Serial.begin(9600);
}

void loop() {
  // put your main code here, to run repeatedly:
  Serial.println((String)"int takes "+sizeof(a)+" Bytes.");
  Serial.println((String)"unsigned int takes "+sizeof(b)+"
  Bytes.");
  Serial.println((String)"short takes "+sizeof(c)+" Bytes.");
  Serial.println((String)"long takes "+sizeof(d)+" Bytes.");
  Serial.println((String)"unsigned long takes "+sizeof(e)+"
  Bytes.");
  Serial.println((String)"byte takes "+sizeof(f)+" Bytes.");
  Serial.println((String)"word takes "+sizeof(g)+" Bytes.");
  Serial.println((String)"float takes "+sizeof(h)+" Bytes.");
  Serial.println((String)"double takes "+sizeof(i)+" Bytes.");
  Serial.println((String)"char takes "+sizeof(j)+" Bytes.");
  Serial.println((String)"bool takes "+sizeof(k)+" Bytes.");
  Serial.println((String)"char array
  {'A','r','d','u','i','n','o'} takes "+sizeof(ch)+" Bytes.");
  Serial.println("-------------------------------");

  delay(60000);
}
```

6.7 Defining Binary and Hexadecimal Variables

The following code shows how binary and hexadecimal variables can be defined. The addition of BIN or HEX to the Serial.print or Serial.println command causes the number to be printed in binary or hexadecimal format, respectively.

```
int a=0b10110010; // You can use int a=0B10110010;
int b=0xC1F;      // You can use int b=0XC1F;

void setup() {
  // put your setup code here, to run once:
  Serial.begin(9600);
}

void loop() {
  // put your main code here, to run repeatedly:
  Serial.println((String)"Value of a in decimal is: "+a);

  Serial.print("Value of a in binary ");
  Serial.println(a,BIN);

  Serial.print("Value of a in Hexadecimal ");
  Serial.println(a,HEX);

  Serial.println();

  Serial.println((String)"Value of b in decimal is: "+b);

  Serial.print("Value of b in binary ");
  Serial.println(b,BIN);
```

```
Serial.print("Value of b in Hexadecimal ");
Serial.println(b,HEX);
Serial.println("-----------------------------");
delay(60000);
}
```

6.8 References for Further Study

[1]   Map function:

https://bit.ly/2HtPHhC

[2]   Arduino data types:

https://bit.ly/3FULbJ5

https://bit.ly/3PRlyNT

[3]   Arduino constants:

https://bit.ly/2Lve1mn

CHAPTER 7

Pulse Width Modulation (PWM)

7.1 Introduction

The duty cycle for a periodic pulse is defined as the ratio of the high section divided by the period. In Figure 7-1, all of the pulses have the same period and frequency; however, their duty cycles are different. When the duty cycle increases, the average and RMS values of the signal increase. For instance, the waveform with a 75% duty cycle has the maximum average and RMS values between the signals shown in Figure 7-1.

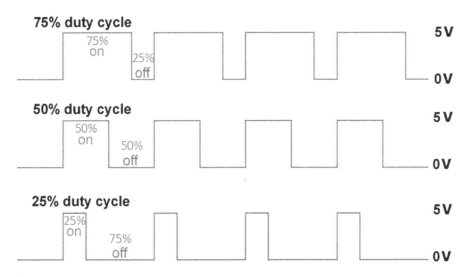

Figure 7-1. *Signals with different duty cycles*

© Farzin Asadi 2023
F. Asadi, *Essentials of Arduino™ Boards Programming*, Maker Innovations Series,
https://doi.org/10.1007/978-1-4842-9600-4_7

RMS and average values for a pulse with a duty ratio of D and a high level of V are equal to $\sqrt{D} \times V$ and $D \times V$, respectively. For instance, RMS and average values of the signal with a 75% duty cycle shown in Figure 7-1 are $\sqrt{D} \times V = \sqrt{0.75} \times 5 = 4.33\ V$ and $D \times V = 0.75 \times 5 = 3.75\ V$, respectively.

Pulse width modulation (PWM) is a method of reducing the average power delivered by an electrical signal by effectively chopping it up into discrete parts. PWM can be used to control the speed of DC motors and intensity of the LED's lights.

Arduino can be used to generate PWM signals. Pins that have a tilde (~) symbol behind them (pins 3, 5, 6, 9, 10, and 11 in Figure 7-2) can be used to generate PWM signals. The frequency of the output waveform for pins 3, 9, 10, and 11 is 490.2 Hz by default. The default PWM frequency for pins 5 and 6 is 976.56 Hz. At the end of this chapter, you will learn how to change this default frequency.

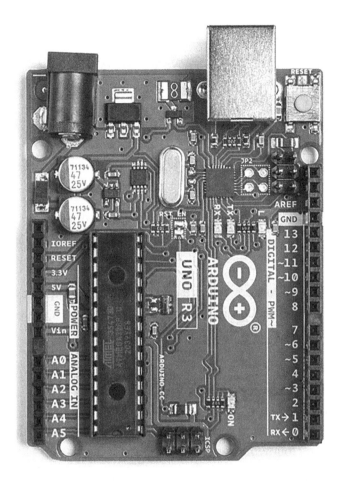

Figure 7-2. *Arduino UNO board*

7.2 PWM Generation on Pin 9

In this example, we want to generate a PWM signal on pin 9 with a duty cycle of 30%. The following code does this job for us. The analogRead command takes two arguments: the PWM pin and required duty cycle. The duty cycle is an integer number between 0 and 255. For instance, if you need a PWM signal with a duty cycle of 30%, you need to give [0.3×255]=[76.5]=76 as the second argument of the analogRead command.

```
//frequency = 490.2 Hz, Duty=30%
float dutyCycle=0.30;
int pwmPin=9;

void setup() {
  // put your setup code here, to run once:
  pinMode(pwmPin, OUTPUT);
}

void loop() {
  // put your main code here, to run repeatedly:
  analogWrite(pwmPin,dutyCycle*255);
}
```

Connect an oscilloscope to pin 9 and measure the frequency and duty cycle of the generated signal. Compare the measured values with the expected ones.

7.3 PWM Generation on Pin 5

In this example, we want to generate a PWM signal on pin 5 with a duty cycle of 30%. The following code does this job for us:

```
//frequency of around 976.56 Hz and dutyCycle of 0.3
float dutyCycle=0.30;
int pwmPin=5;

void setup() {
  // put your setup code here, to run once:
  pinMode(pwmPin, OUTPUT);
}
```

```
void loop() {
  // put your main code here, to run repeatedly:
  analogWrite(pwmPin,dutyCycle*255);
}
```

Connect an oscilloscope to pin 5 and measure the frequency and duty cycle of the generated signal. Compare the measured values with the expected ones.

7.4 Duty Cycle Control with Potentiometer

In the previous examples, the duty cycle was constant and equal to the value entered into the code. In this example, we will use a potentiometer to set the duty cycle of the generated PWM signal. When the potentiometer shaft is turned, the voltage of the center terminal changes from 0 V up to 5 V. We read the ADC and use the reading to determine the duty cycle of the PWM signal. Note that the analogRead command accepts values from 0 to 255 for the duty cycle; however, the value that comes from the ADC is in the [0, 1023] interval. If we divide the number that comes from the ADC by 4, it goes into the [0, 255] interval which is what we want.

```
//frequency = 490 Hz
int pwmPin=9;

void setup() {
  // put your setup code here, to run once:
  pinMode(pwmPin, OUTPUT);
}

void loop() {
  // put your main code here, to run repeatedly:
  analogWrite(pwmPin,analogRead(A0)/4);
}
```

The hardware of this example is shown in Figure 7-3. Connect pin 9 to an oscilloscope and ensure that the duty cycle changes when turning the potentiometer shaft.

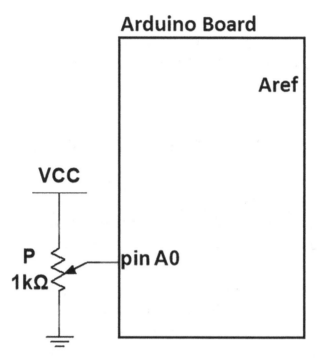

Figure 7-3. *Hardware of the studied example*

You can use the generated PWM signal to control the speed of a small DC motor (Figure 7-4). Increasing the duty cycle of the PWM signal increases the speed of the motor.

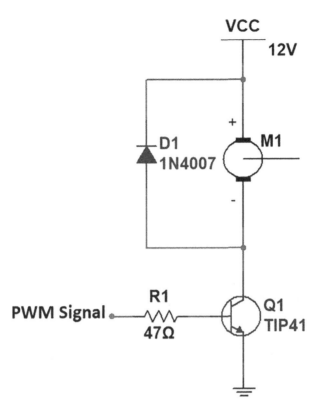

Figure 7-4. *Control of a DC motor speed*

7.5 Control the Intensity of an LED

In the previous example, you learned how to use the PWM signal in order to control a small DC motor. In this example, we will use the PWM signal to control the intensity of an LED. A higher duty cycle means a higher light intensity.

In the following code, the duty cycle of the PWM signal increases with time. After reaching the maximum value, the duty cycle starts to decrease. Decrease with time continues until the duty cycle reaches its minimum. After reaching the minimum, the duty cycle starts to increase again, and this cycle continues.

```
int LED=9;
int Delay=30;
int dutyCycle=0;

void setup() {
  // put your setup code here, to run once:
  pinMode(LED,OUTPUT);
}

void loop() {
  // put your main code here, to run repeatedly:
  dutyCycle=0;
  for (int i=0;i<17;i++){
    dutyCycle=dutyCycle+15;
    analogWrite(LED,dutyCycle);
    delay(Delay);
  }

  for (int j=0;j<17;j++){
    dutyCycle=dutyCycle-15;
    analogWrite(LED,dutyCycle);
    delay(Delay);
  }

  delay(500);
}
```

The hardware of this example is shown in Figure 7-5. After uploading the code, the LED starts to blink smoothly.

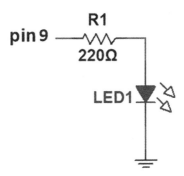

Figure 7-5. *Hardware of the studied example*

The code of this example can be written with the aid of functions as well. In the following code, the fade function turns on and off the LED smoothly:

```
int LED=9;
int Delay=30;
int dutyCycle=0;

void setup() {
  // put your setup code here, to run once:
  pinMode(LED,OUTPUT);
}

void loop() {
  // put your main code here, to run repeatedly:
  fade(3);
  delay(2000);
}

void fade(int n){
for (int k=1;k<=n;k++){
  dutyCycle=0;
  for (int i=0;i<17;i++){
```

```
    dutyCycle=dutyCycle+15;
    analogWrite(LED,dutyCycle);
    delay(Delay);
  }

  for (int j=0;j<17;j++){
    dutyCycle=dutyCycle-15;
    analogWrite(LED,dutyCycle);
    delay(Delay);
  }

  delay(500);
}
}
```

7.6 Change the Frequency of the PWM Signal

Tables 7-1 to 7-3 show the required codes to change the frequency of the generated PWM signal. Only the frequencies shown in the tables are available. The frequency of the PWM signal taken from pin 5 is equal to the frequency of the PWM signal taken from pin D6. In other words, we cannot have two different frequencies on pins D5 and D6. Frequencies of these two pins are always equal to each other. The same rule is correct for D9-D1 and D3-D11 couples.

Table 7-1. *Codes to change the PWM frequency of pins D5 and D6*

Frequency (Hz)	Required Code
62500.00	TCCR0B = TCCR0B & B11111000 | B00000001;
7812.50	TCCR0B = TCCR0B & B11111000 | B00000010;
976.56 (Default)	TCCR0B = TCCR0B & B11111000 | B00000011;
244.14	TCCR0B = TCCR0B & B11111000 | B00000100;
61.04	TCCR0B = TCCR0B & B11111000 | B00000101;

Table 7-2. *Codes to change the PWM frequency of pins D9 and D10*

Frequency (Hz)	Required Code
31372.55	TCCR1B = TCCR1B & B11111000 | B00000001;
3921.16	TCCR1B = TCCR1B & B11111000 | B00000010;
490.20 (Default)	TCCR1B = TCCR1B & B11111000 | B00000011;
122.55	TCCR1B = TCCR1B & B11111000 | B00000100;
30.64	TCCR1B = TCCR1B & B11111000 | B00000101;

Table 7-3. *Codes to change the PWM frequency of pins D3 and D11*

Frequency (Hz)	Required Code
31372.55	TCCR2B = TCCR2B & B11111000 | B00000001;
3921.16	TCCR2B = TCCR2B & B11111000 | B00000010;
980.39	TCCR2B = TCCR2B & B11111000 | B00000011;
490.20 (Default)	TCCR2B = TCCR2B & B11111000 | B00000100;
245.10	TCCR2B = TCCR2B & B11111000 | B00000101;
122.55	TCCR2B = TCCR2B & B11111000 | B00000110;
30.64	TCCR2B = TCCR2B & B11111000 | B00000111;

Let's study an example to see how these tables can be used. For instance, assume that we want to generate a PWM signal with a frequency of 31.372 kHz and a duty cycle of 30% on pin 9 of the Arduino board. The following code does this job for us:

```
//frequency of around 31.372 kHz and dutyCycle of 0.3
float dutyCycle=0.30;
int pwmPin=9;

void setup() {
  // put your setup code here, to run once:
  pinMode(pwmPin, OUTPUT);
  TCCR1B = TCCR1B & B11111000 | B00000001;
}

void loop() {
  // put your main code here, to run repeatedly:
  analogWrite(pwmPin,dutyCycle*255);
}
```

You can connect an oscilloscope to pin 9 and ensure that the generated waveform is what we expect.

7.7 References for Further Study

[1]   Basics of PWM:

https://bit.ly/3GjFq94

https://bit.ly/3vitkao

CHAPTER 8

Control of Different Types of Motors

8.1 Introduction

Motors are building blocks of many projects. This chapter shows how different types of motors can be controlled with an Arduino board.

8.2 Control of Servo Motor

In this example, we want to control a small servo motor (SG90 model). The servo motor has three wires: red, brown, and orange. The red and brown wires are the motor supply, and the orange wire is the signal which controls the position of the shaft.

Upload the following code to the board. This code reads the voltage of analog pin A0 and rotates the shaft of the servo motor with respect to the voltage applied to pin A0:

```
int shaftAngle=0;

#include <Servo.h>
Servo servo1;
```

© Farzin Asadi 2023
F. Asadi, *Essentials of Arduino™ Boards Programming*, Maker Innovations Series,
https://doi.org/10.1007/978-1-4842-9600-4_8

```
void setup() {
  // put your setup code here, to run once:
  servo1.attach(9);
  Serial.begin(9600);
}

void loop() {
  // put your main code here, to run repeatedly:
  shaftAngle=map(analogRead(A0),0,1023,0,180);
  servo1.write(shaftAngle);
  Serial.println((String)"Given command: "+shaftAngle);
  delay(100);
}
```

The hardware of this example is shown in Figure 8-1. Figure 8-2 shows a better and more reliable way to drive the servo motor. In Figure 8-2, the supply of the servo motor is taken from an external power source. Note that the ground of an external source must be connected to the ground of the Arduino board. Using an external power source avoids drawing the motor current from the Arduino board. In the schematic shown in Figure 8-1, the motor may draw a high current from the Arduino board. Such a high current may destroy the voltage regulator on the Arduino board.

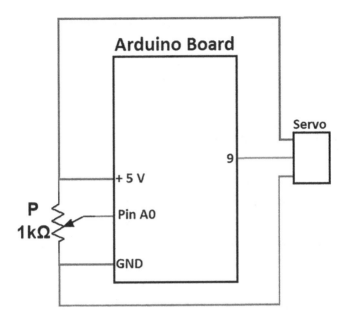

Figure 8-1. *Hardware of the studied example*

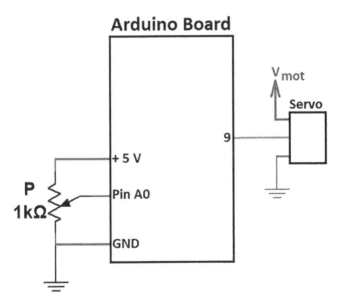

Figure 8-2. *Preferred hardware for the studied example*

The SG90 servo motor without any load makes no problem for the Arduino board shown in Figure 8-1. Therefore, you can use the schematic shown in Figure 8-1. The shaft of the motor rotates when you rotate the potentiometer shaft.

8.3 Control of BLDC

In this section, we want to control the speed of a Brushless Direct Current (BLDC) motor. You need a driver in order to control the speed of a BLDC motor. The driver has eight wires: two wires for motor supply, three wires for connecting the motor windings to the driver, and three wires for taking the control signals. These three wires are connected to the Arduino board. The three wires that reconnected to the Arduino have red, brown, and orange colors. Red and brown supply the driver board, and the control signal is applied to the orange terminal. Red, brown, and orange wires are thin; other wires are thick.

Upload the following code to the board:

```
/*
        Arduino Brushless Motor Control
*/

#include <Servo.h>

Servo ESC;      // create servo object to control the ESC

int potValue;   // value from the analog pin

void setup() {
  // Attach the ESC on pin 9
  ESC.attach(9,1000,2000); // (pin, min pulse width, max pulse
  width in microseconds)
}
```

```
void loop() {
  potValue = analogRead(A0);   // reads the value of the
  potentiometer (value between 0 and 1023)
  potValue = map(potValue, 0, 1023, 0, 180);   // scale it to
  use it with the servo library (value between 0 and 180)
  ESC.write(potValue);   // Send the signal to the ESC
}
```

The hardware of this example is shown in Figure 8-3. You can change the speed of the BLDC motor with the aid of the potentiometer P1.

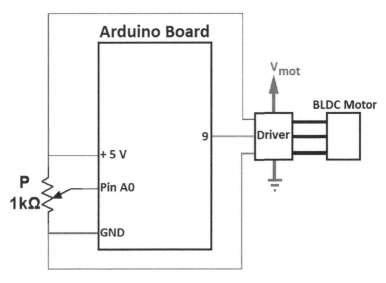

Figure 8-3. *Hardware of the studied example*

8.4 Control of Stepper motor with A4988 Driver

Stepper motors require a driver in order to work with the Arduino board. Allegro A4988 is one of the most commonly used Stepper motor driver ICs. A4988 has a maximum output capacity of 35 V and ±2 A which is great for driving small- to medium-sized Stepper motors like NEMA 17 bipolar stepper motor. A driver board based on this IC is shown in Figure 8-4.

229

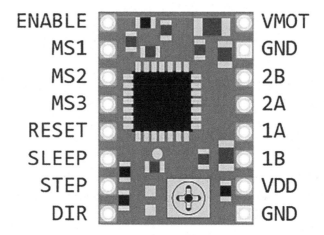

Figure 8-4. *A4988-based driver board*

Stepper motors typically have a step size of 1.8° or 200 steps per revolution; this refers to full steps. A microstepping driver such as the A4988 allows higher resolutions by allowing intermediate step locations. This is achieved by energizing the coils with intermediate current levels. For instance, driving a motor in quarter-step mode will give the 200-step-per-revolution motor 800 microsteps per revolution by using four different current levels. The resolution (step size) selector pins (MS1, MS2, and MS3) allow you to select one of the five step resolutions according to Table 8-1. When you leave MS1, MS2, and MS3 unconnected, the motor is in full step as well.

Table 8-1. *Step size selection*

MS1	MS2	MS3	Microstep Resolution
Low	Low	Low	Full step
High	Low	Low	1/2 step
Low	High	Low	1/4 step
High	High	Low	1/8 step
High	High	High	1/16 step

The following code rotates the Stepper motor shaft one revolution in the clockwise direction and one revolution in the counterclockwise direction. Upload the code to the board:

```
/*Example sketch to control a stepper motor with A4988 stepper
motor driver and Arduino without a library.*/

// Define stepper motor connections and steps per revolution:
#define dirPin 2
#define stepPin 3
#define stepsPerRevolution 200
#define Delay 1000 //For a fast motion use 500.

void setup() {
  // Declare pins as output:
  pinMode(stepPin, OUTPUT);
  pinMode(dirPin, OUTPUT);
}

void loop() {
  // Set the spinning direction clockwise:
  Rotate(200);         //Rotate the motor 1 revolution
  delay(500);
  RotateReverse(200); //Rotate the motor 1 revolution in the
                          reverse direction
  delay(500);
}

void Rotate(int numberOfSteps){
    digitalWrite(dirPin, HIGH);

    for (int i = 0; i <numberOfSteps; i++) {
    // These four lines result in 1 step:
    digitalWrite(stepPin, HIGH);
    delayMicroseconds(Delay);
```

```
    digitalWrite(stepPin, LOW);
    delayMicroseconds(Delay);
  }
}

void RotateReverse(int numberOfSteps){
    digitalWrite(dirPin, LOW);

    for (int i = 0; i <numberOfSteps; i++) {
    // These four lines result in 1 step:
    digitalWrite(stepPin, HIGH);
    delayMicroseconds(Delay);
    digitalWrite(stepPin, LOW);
    delayMicroseconds(Delay);
  }
}
```

The hardware of this example is shown in Figure 8-5. Note that the power of the motor is taken from a separate source.

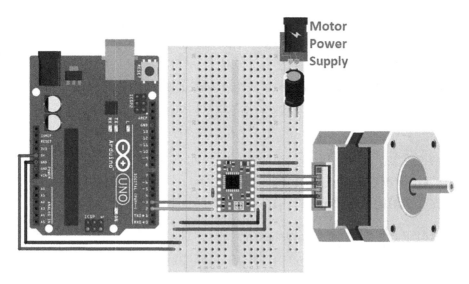

Figure 8-5. *Hardware of the studied example*

8.5 Control of 28BYJ-48 5V Stepper motor

In this example, we will see how a 28BYJ-48 Stepper motor can be controlled with the Arduino board. 28BYJ-48 is a cheap high torque Stepper motor which is suitable for many applications. It has a gearbox with a reduction ratio of around 64 inside the motor case.

28BYJ-48 requires a driver like other Stepper motors. ULN2003 IC can be used to drive this motor. The 28BYJ-48 Stepper motor and its driver are shown in Figure 8-6.

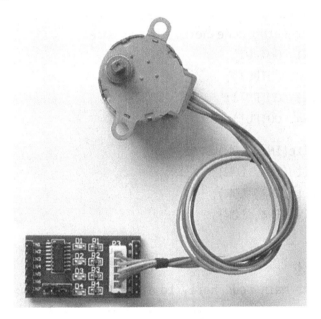

Figure 8-6. *28BYJ-48 5V Stepper motor and its driver board*

Upload the following code to the Arduino board. This code rotates the shaft one revolution in the clockwise direction, waits for one second, rotates the shaft one revolution in the counterclockwise direction, waits for one second, and repeats this process.

```
//Stepper motor 28BYJ-48
//Driver ULN2003 module
//https://www.youtube.com/watch?v=avrdDZD7qEQ

#define IN1 8
#define IN2 9
#define IN3 10
#define IN4 11
#define Delay 2

void setup() {
  // put your setup code here, to run once:
  pinMode(IN1, OUTPUT);
  pinMode(IN2, OUTPUT);
  pinMode(IN3, OUTPUT);
  pinMode(IN4, OUTPUT);

  digitalWrite(IN1, LOW);
  digitalWrite(IN2, LOW);
  digitalWrite(IN3, LOW);
  digitalWrite(IN4, LOW);
}

void loop() {
  // put your main code here, to run repeatedly:
  Rotate(512); // Rotates the shaft 1 full revolution
  delay(1000);
  RotateReverse(512);
  delay(1000);
}

void Rotate(int n){
  for (int i=0;i<n;i++){
    digitalWrite(IN1,HIGH);
```

```
    delay(Delay);
    digitalWrite(IN1,LOW);

    digitalWrite(IN2,HIGH);
    delay(Delay);
    digitalWrite(IN2,LOW);

    digitalWrite(IN3,HIGH);
    delay(Delay);
    digitalWrite(IN3,LOW);

    digitalWrite(IN4,HIGH);
    delay(Delay);
    digitalWrite(IN4,LOW);
  }
}

void RotateReverse(int n){
  for (int i=0;i<n;i++){
    digitalWrite(IN4,HIGH);
    delay(Delay);
    digitalWrite(IN4,LOW);

    digitalWrite(IN3,HIGH);
    delay(Delay);
    digitalWrite(IN3,LOW);

    digitalWrite(IN2,HIGH);
    delay(Delay);
    digitalWrite(IN2,LOW);

    digitalWrite(IN1,HIGH);
    delay(Delay);
    digitalWrite(IN1,LOW);
  }
}
```

The hardware of this example is shown in Figure 8-7. The + and – terminals of the driver board are connected to the power supply of the Stepper motor (this motor is designed for 5 V supply). Ensure that the two terminals behind the <-> symbol must be connected to each other.

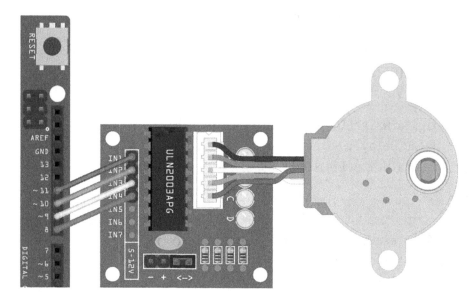

Figure 8-7. *Hardware of the studied example*

8.6 Control of DC Motor

DC motors can be controlled easily with DC motor drivers like VNH3ASP30, L298, and L293 ICs. For instance, a DC motor driver board which uses the L293 IC is shown in Figure 8-8.

Figure 8-8. *L293D-based DC motor driver*

Working with DC motor driver boards is quite easy. Nearly all of the DC motor drivers use the same interface. All of the DC motor driver boards are composed of the following pins:

1) **Motor supply voltage terminals**: The energy of the motor is supplied from these pins.

2) **IC supply voltage terminals**: The energy of the IC on the board is supplied from these pins. Generally, these pins are connected to the +5 and ground of the microcontroller board.

3) **PWM terminals**: These pins generally have an EN label behind them. With the aid of the PWM, you can control the speed or position of the motor's shaft. These pins are connected to the microcontroller board.

4) **Direction terminals**: These two pins generally have IN1 and IN2 labels behind them. With the aid of these pins, you can determine the direction of rotation and break the shaft. For instance, when IN1=High and IN2=Low, the motor rotates clockwise; when IN1=Low and IN2=High, the motor rotates counterclockwise; and when IN1=Low and IN2=Low, the motor brakes. These two pins are connected to the microcontroller board.

5) **Motor terminals**: The DC motor is connected to the driver using these two pins.

For instance, connections of the L293-based DC motor driver board are shown in Figure 8-9. DC9-24V is used to supply the energy to the DC motors. This board can drive two DC motors. Therefore, it has four direction pins: IN1 and IN2 for one of the motors and IN3 and IN4 for the other one. DC5V shows the supply voltage for the IC on the board. MOTOR 1 and MOTOR 2 show the terminals that are connected to the DC motors. EN1 and EN2 show the PWM terminals that control the motor 1 and motor 2, respectively. Note that these pins are connected to the upper pin using a jumper (Figure 8-10). Generally, +5 V pins are behind the PWM pins, and the jumper connects the PWM pin to the +5 V. When the jumper connects the PWM terminal to +5 V, the DC motor sees a PWM signal with a duty cycle of 100%. In other words, when the jumper connects the PWM terminal to +5 V, the motor runs with a maximum speed which may not be interesting in many applications. You need to remove the jumper and connect the PWM pin to the microcontroller board in order to be able to control the speed and position of the shaft. PWM is set by the code that you wrote. The speed of the motor is directly proportional to the duty cycle of the PWM signal applied to the driver.

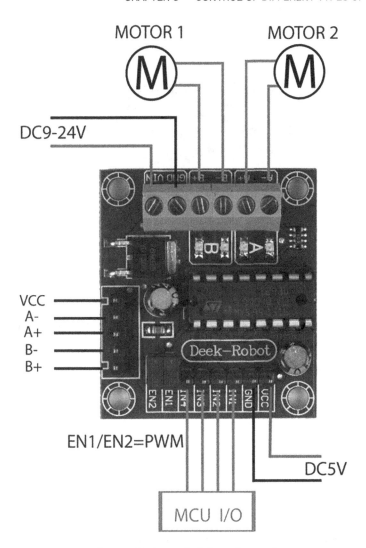

Figure 8-9. *Pinout of L293D-based driver board*

Figure 8-10. *Jumpers of L293D-based driver board*

Let's study an example. In the following code, the motor rotates in one direction with half of its maximum speed, then stops, then rotates in the reverse direction with maximum speed. IN1, IN2, and EN1 pins of the DC motor driver board are connected to pins 8, 9, and 10 of the Arduino board, respectively.

```
#define IN1 8
#define IN2 9
#define EN 10

void setup() {
  // put your setup code here, to run once:
  pinMode(IN1,OUTPUT);
  pinMode(IN2,OUTPUT);
  pinMode(EN,OUTPUT);
}
```

```
void loop() {
  // put your main code here, to run repeatedly:

    digitalWrite(IN1,HIGH);
    digitalWrite(IN2,LOW);
    analogWrite(EN,125);
    delay(3000);

    digitalWrite(IN1,LOW);
    digitalWrite(IN2,LOW);
    delay(1000);

    digitalWrite(IN1,LOW);
    digitalWrite(IN2,HIGH);
    analogWrite(EN,250);
    delay(3000);
}
```

8.7 Reading an Encoder

An encoder is used to convert the angular position or motion of a shaft to
digital output signals. Encoders are used for closed loop control of electric
motors (Figure 8-11). Some types of encoders are used as input devices
and permit the Arduino to take some variables from the user (Figure 8-12).
For instance, in Figure 8-1 we used a potentiometer to control the shaft
of a servo motor. You can replace the potentiometer with an encoder. In
this case, the servo motor moves clockwise when the shaft of the encoder
is rotated clockwise and moves counterclockwise when the shaft of the
encoder is rotated counterclockwise. Refer to the references given at the
end of this chapter if you are not familiar with the working principle of
encoders.

Figure 8-11. *A typical encoder used in closed loop control of electric motors*

Figure 8-12. *Small encoder suitable for entering a variable to the microcontroller*

The following code uses the Encoder library to read an encoder:

```
//visit: http://www.pjrc.com/teensy/td_libs_Encoder.html
//Download the library from https://github.com/
PaulStoffregen/Encoder

#include <Encoder.h>

// Change these two numbers to the pins connected to your
   encoder.
//   Best Performance: both pins have interrupt capability
//   Good Performance: only the first pin has interrupt
     capability
//   Low Performance:  neither pin has interrupt capability
Encoder myEnc(5, 6);
//   avoid using pins with LEDs attached

void setup() {
  Serial.begin(9600);
  Serial.println("Basic Encoder Test:");
}

long oldPosition  = -999;

void loop() {
  long newPosition = myEnc.read();
  if (newPosition != oldPosition) {
    oldPosition = newPosition;
    Serial.println(newPosition);
  }
}
```

The hardware of this example is shown in Figure 8-13. After uploading the code to the Arduino board, rotate the encoder clockwise and counterclockwise and see the output using the Serial Monitor.

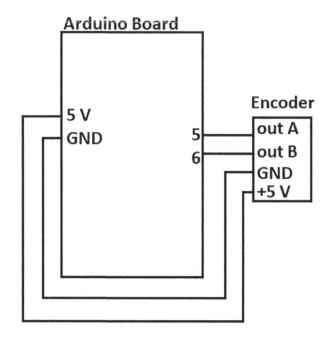

Figure 8-13. *Hardware of the studied example*

If you don't have an encoder, you can use the simple circuit shown in Figure 8-14. The clock can come from a fancy function generator or a cheap 555 timer chip. The frequencies of OutA and OutB are equal to each other; however, there exists a 90° of phase difference between them. The frequency of the output is one fourth of the frequency of the input clock.

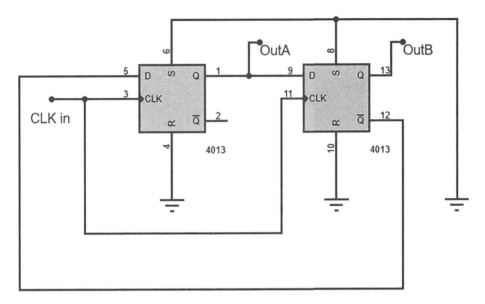

Figure 8-14. *A circuit to emulate quadrature encoder signals*

8.8 Control of Servo Motor with Encoder

In this example, we want to replace the potentiometer in Figure 8-2 with an encoder. We want to control the position of the servo motor shaft by rotating the encoder. Upload the following code to the Arduino board:

```
int shaftAngle=0;

#include <Encoder.h>
#include <Servo.h>

Encoder myEnc(5, 6);
Servo servo1;
long oldPosition  = -999;
```

```
void setup() {
  // put your setup code here, to run once:
  servo1.attach(9);
  Serial.begin(9600);
}

void loop() {
  // write command is explained in https://www.pjrc.com/teensy/
    td_libs_Encoder.html
  long newPosition = myEnc.read();
  //following two lines force the encoder to generate a number
    between 0 and 1800.
  if (newPosition<0) myEnc.write(0);
  if (newPosition>1800) myEnc.write(1800);

  if (newPosition != oldPosition){
    oldPosition = newPosition;
    Serial.println(newPosition);
  }

  shaftAngle=(newPosition/10); //decrease the movement of
                                    the shaft
  servo1.write(shaftAngle);
}
```

The hardware of this example is shown in Figure 8-15. After uploading the code to the board, open the Serial Monitor and rotate the encoder to move the servo motor's shaft.

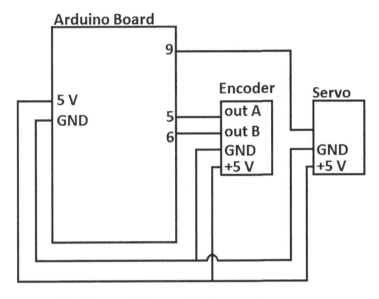

Figure 8-15. *Hardware of the studied example*

8.9 References for Further Study

[1]   A4988 datasheet:

https://bit.ly/3vjjCnU

[2]   Stepper motor control with A4988:

https://bit.ly/3Il1dPt

[3]   Datasheet of 28BYJ-48 5V stepper motor:

https://bit.ly/3VrmEkG

[4]   BLDC motor control with Arduino:

https://bit.ly/2Ga9wOD

[5]   BLDC KV rating:

https://bit.ly/3FNjLVu

[6]   Encoder:

https://bit.ly/3PTOqa7

https://bit.ly/2U3JSm3

CHAPTER 9

Interrupts and Internal Comparator

9.1 Introduction

An interrupt is a signal emitted by hardware or software when a process or an event needs immediate attention. It alerts the processor to a high priority process requiring interruption of the current working process. When the event or interrupt happens, the processor takes immediate notice, saves its execution state, runs a small chunk of code (Interrupt Service Routine, ISR), and then returns back to whatever it was doing before.

Consider a case; while a car is running, the microcontroller is busy sensing the speed of the car, checking other sensors, controlling the air conditioner temperature, etc. But suddenly an accident happened! At that time, the controller stops all the works and goes to the airbag activation section. So what makes a sudden opening of airbag in seconds? An interrupt signal is used here which has the highest priority of all.

© Farzin Asadi 2023
F. Asadi, *Essentials of Arduino™ Boards Programming*, Maker Innovations Series,
https://doi.org/10.1007/978-1-4842-9600-4_9

There are software and hardware interrupts:

> **Hardware interrupts**: These occur in response to an external event, like a pin going high or low. Only pins 2 and 3 can be used for hardware interrupts in Arduino UNO, Nano, Mini, and other ATmega328-based boards.

> **Software interrupts**: These occur in response to a software instruction.

This chapter helps you to understand the concept of interrupt.

9.2 Simple Frequency Meter

In this example, we want to make a simple frequency meter to measure the frequency of pulses. If you want to measure the frequency of sinusoidal signals, you need to convert them into a square wave with the aid of a Schmitt trigger. In this section, we assume that our input signal is a pulse with a high level of +5 V and low level of 0 V.

The following code takes the input signal from pin 2 of Arduino. Each time pin 2 goes from low to high, ISR_MeasureFreq is called. ISR_MeasureFreq sets the value of t1. Variable t1 shows the time instant of the last rising edge of the signal under measurement. Variable t0 shows the time instant of the previous rising edge of the signal under measurement. The time difference between t1 and t0 is one period. Therefore, the frequency is 1/(t1-t0).

```
unsigned long t0=0;
volatile unsigned long t1=0;
bool b=false;
```

```
void setup() {
  // put your setup code here, to run once:
  Serial.begin(115200);
  pinMode(9,OUTPUT);
  analogWrite(9,122);

  pinMode(2,INPUT);
  attachInterrupt(digitalPinToInterrupt(2),ISR_
  measureFreq,RISING);
}

void loop() {
  // put your main code here, to run repeatedly:
  if (b){
    Serial.println((String)"Freq. is: "+ 1E6/(t1-t0) +" Hz.");
    t0=t1;
    b=false;
  }
}

void ISR_measureFreq(){
  t1=micros();
  b=true;
}
```

The preceding code generates a PWM signal with a duty cycle of $122/255 = 0.5$ or 50% on pin 9 of the Arduino board. You can use the generated PWM signal as a test signal (Figure 9-1).

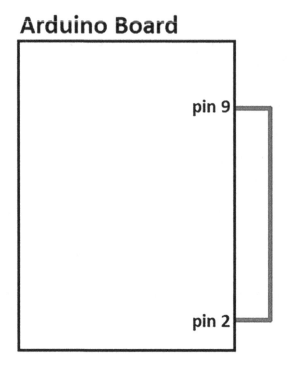

Figure 9-1. *Hardware of the studied example*

After uploading the code and connecting pin 2 to 9, open the Serial Monitor to see the result of measurement (Figure 9-2).

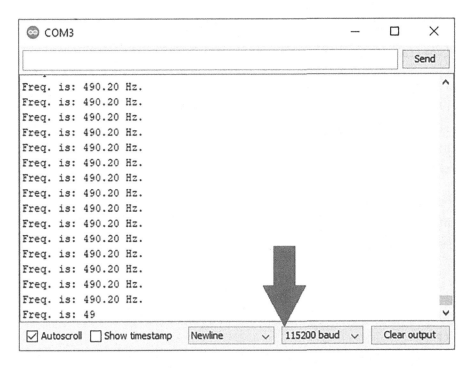

Figure 9-2. *Sample output*

9.3 Improved Simple Frequency Meter

The code given in the previous section prints the frequency many times per second. Let's decrease the number of prints to one time per second.

The following code prints the result once per deltaT millisecond. Variable deltaT is 1000; therefore, the result will be printed once per 1000 ms, which is equal to once per second.

```
unsigned long t0=0;
volatile unsigned long t1=0;
bool b=false;

unsigned long t2;
```

```
unsigned long t3;

int deltaT=1000;

void setup() {
  // put your setup code here, to run once:
  Serial.begin(115200);
  pinMode(9,OUTPUT);
  analogWrite(9,122);

  pinMode(2,INPUT);
  attachInterrupt(digitalPinToInterrupt(2),ISR_
  measureFreq,RISING);
}

void loop() {
  // put your main code here, to run repeatedly:
  if (b){
    t3=millis();
    if ((t3-t2)>deltaT){
      Serial.println((String)"Freq. is: "+ 1E6/(t1-t0));
      t2=t3;
    }
    t0=t1;
    b=false;
  }
}

void ISR_measureFreq(){
  t1=micros();
  b=true;
}
```

The preceding code generates a PWM signal with a duty cycle of 122/255=0.5 or 50% on pin 9 of the Arduino board. You can use the generated PWM signal as a test signal (Figure 9-3).

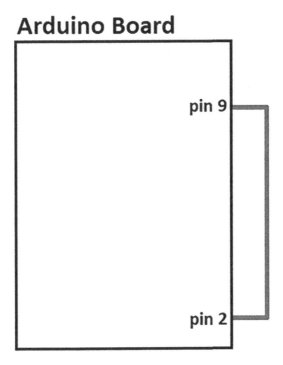

Figure 9-3. *Hardware of the studied example*

After uploading the code and connecting pin 2 to 9, open the Serial Monitor to see the result of measurement.

9.4 Frequency Measurement with the FreqCount Library

In this example, we will use the FreqCount library to measure the frequency of a pulse applied to pin 5 of Arduino UNO. Upload the following code to the board:

```
//Download the library from https://github.com/PaulStoffregen/
FreqCount/archive/master.zip
// input signal must be applied to pin 5 of Arduino UNO, 12 of
Leonardo or 47 of MEGA
#include <FreqCount.h>

void setup() {
  Serial.begin(9600);
  FreqCount.begin(1000); //counts the number of pulses in
                          1000 ms.
}

void loop() {
  if (FreqCount.available()) {
    unsigned long count = FreqCount.read();
    Serial.println((String)"Frequency is: "+count+"Hz.");
  }
}
```

Use the Serial Monitor to see the output of this code.

9.5 pulseIn Command

In this example, we want to use the pulseIn command to measure the duration of high (tH) and low (tL) sections of a pulse (you can use this method to measure frequency as well since $f=1/T=1/(tH+tL)$). Upload the following code to the Arduino board:

```
// Pulse width measurement
// https://www.arduino.cc/reference/en/language/functions/
advanced-io/pulsein/
#define pin 7
unsigned long posDuration=0;
unsigned long negDuration=0;
```

```
void setup() {
  // put your setup code here, to run once:
  Serial.begin(9600);
  pinMode(pin,INPUT);
}

void loop() {
  posDuration=pulseIn(pin,HIGH); //reads the positive width in
                                  micro seconds
  negDuration=pulseIn(pin,LOW);  //reads the positive width in
                                  micro seconds

  Serial.println((String)"Length of positive
  section:"+posDuration);
  Serial.println((String)"Length of negative
  section:"+negDuration);
  Serial.println();

  delay(1000);
}
```

Apply the signal under measurement to pin 7 of Arduino. Open the Serial Monitor to see the output of the code.

9.6 Triggering an Interrupt with a Push Button

In this section, we want to use a push button connected to pin 2 to trigger the interrupt. In the following code, pin 2 is pulled up to VCC with the aid of an internal pull-up resistor. When the user presses the push button, the button connects pin 2 to ground. At the instant that the pin goes from high (+5 V) to low (0 V), we have a falling edge. This falling edge is used to trigger an interrupt. ISR is written in the LEDblink function. This function forces the onboard LED to blink three times. The LED is on for 500 ms, and it is off for 500 ms.

```
unsigned long t0=0;
unsigned long t1=0;
volatile unsigned long n=0;

void setup() {
  // put your setup code here, to run once:
  Serial.begin(9600);
  pinMode(13,OUTPUT);
  digitalWrite(13,LOW);
  pinMode(2,INPUT_PULLUP);
  attachInterrupt(digitalPinToInterrupt(2),LEDblink,FALLING);
}

void loop() {
  // put your main code here, to run repeatedly:
  Serial.println(n);
}

void LEDblink(){
  n++;
  for (int i=0;i<3;i++){
    digitalWrite(13, HIGH);
    for (int j=0;j<500;j++)
      delayMicroseconds(1000);

    digitalWrite(13, LOW);
    for (int k=0;k<500;k++)
      delayMicroseconds(1000);
  }
}
```

Upload the code to the Arduino board. The hardware is shown in Figure 9-4. The onboard LED starts to blink at the instant that you press the push button.

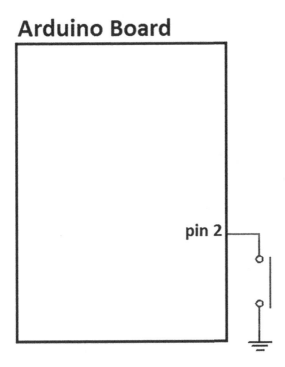

Figure 9-4. *Hardware of the studied example*

As an exercise, edit the preceding code to blink the LED when you release the push button.

9.7 Triggering an Interrupt with Level

In the previous sections, we used the edge in order to trigger the interrupt. The interrupt can be triggered with the aid of a level as well. In Arduino UNO, you can trigger an interrupt with a low level. This means that the interrupt is triggered when the pin is low. The DUE, Zero, and MKR1000 boards permit you to trigger an interrupt on a high level as well.

In the following code, the onboard LED blinks three times when the user presses the push button:

```
unsigned long t0=0;
unsigned long t1=0;
volatile unsigned long n=0;

void setup() {
  // put your setup code here, to run once:
  Serial.begin(9600);
  pinMode(13,OUTPUT);
  digitalWrite(13,LOW);
  pinMode(2,INPUT_PULLUP);
  attachInterrupt(digitalPinToInterrupt(2),LEDblink,LOW);
}

void loop() {
  // put your main code here, to run repeatedly:
  Serial.println(n);
}

void LEDblink(){
  n++;
  for (int i=0;i<3;i++){
    digitalWrite(13, HIGH);
    for (int j=0;j<500;j++)
      delayMicroseconds(1000);

    digitalWrite(13, LOW);
    for (int k=0;k<500;k++)
      delayMicroseconds(1000);
  }
}
```

The hardware of this example is shown in Figure 9-5.

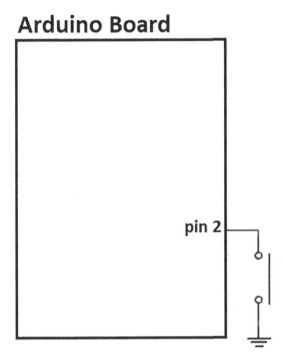

Figure 9-5. *Hardware of the studied example*

9.8 Comparator Interrupt

ATmega328 has an internal comparator which permits you to do analog comparisons without any need to external Op Amps or comparator IC.

A block diagram of the internal comparator is shown in Figure 9-6 (Figure 9-6, Figures 9-8 to 9-12, and Tables 9-1 and 9-2 are taken from [1]. The label above figures/tables shows the label of the figure/table in the original reference).

Figure 22-1. Analog Comparator Block Diagram[2]

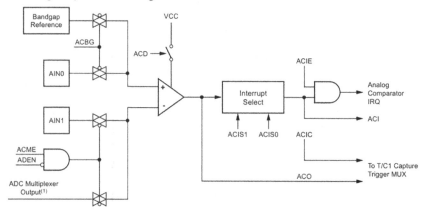

Figure 9-6. *Block diagram of the analog comparator*

The analog comparator compares the input values on the positive pin AIN0 and negative pin AIN1. When the voltage on the positive pin AIN0 is higher than the voltage on the negative pin AIN1, the analog comparator output, ACO, is set. The comparator's output can be set to trigger the Timer/Counter1 input capture function. In addition, the comparator can trigger a separate interrupt, exclusive to the analog comparator. The user can select interrupt triggering on the comparator output rise, fall, or toggle.

As shown in Figure 9-7, pins AIN0 and AIN1 of the analog comparator module are externally connected to the I/O pins PD6 (pin 6 of the Arduino UNO board) and PD7 (pin 7 of the Arduino UNO board).

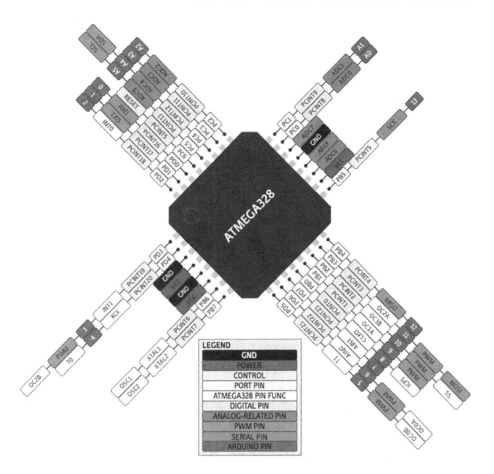

Figure 9-7. *Connection between ATmega328 microcontroller pins and Arduino UNO pins*

Even though AIN0 is fixed as one of the inputs, AIN1 can be varied using the ADMUX output as shown in Table 9-1. If ACME is cleared or ADEN is set, AIN1 is applied to the negative input of the analog comparator.

Table 9-1. *Selection of desired source for the negative input of the comparator*

Table 22-1. Analog Comparator Multiplexed Input

ACME	ADEN	MUX2..0	Analog Comparator Negative Input
0	x	xxx	AIN1
1	1	xxx	AIN1
1	0	000	ADC0
1	0	001	ADC1
1	0	010	ADC2
1	0	011	ADC3
1	0	100	ADC4
1	0	101	ADC5
1	0	110	ADC6
1	0	111	ADC7

9.9 Important Registers of the Internal Analog Comparator

The internal comparator's important registers and important bits of the registers are studied in this section.

The ADCSRA register is shown in Figure 9-8.

23.9.2 ADCSRA – ADC Control and Status Register A

Bit	7	6	5	4	3	2	1	0	
(0x7A)	ADEN	ADSC	ADATE	ADIF	ADIE	ADPS2	ADPS1	ADPS0	ADCSRA
Read/Write	R/W	R/W	R/W	R/W	R/W	R/W	R/W	R/W	
Initial Value	0	0	0	0	0	0	0	0	

Figure 9-8. *Bits of the ADCSRA register*

ADEN bit (ADC Enable): Writing this bit to one enables the ADC. By writing it to zero, the ADC is turned off. Turning the ADC off while a conversion is in progress will terminate this conversion.

The ADCSRB register is shown in Figure 9-9.

22.3.1 ADCSRB – ADC Control and Status Register B

Bit	7	6	5	4	3	2	1	0	
(0x7B)	–	ACME	–	–	–	ADTS2	ADTS1	ADTS0	ADCSRB
Read/Write	R	R/W	R	R	R	R/W	R/W	R/W	
Initial Value	0	0	0	0	0	0	0	0	

Figure 9-9. *Bits of the ADCSRB register*

ACME bit (Analog Comparator Multiplexer Enable): When this bit is written logic one and the ADC is switched off (ADEN in ADCSRA is zero), the ADC multiplexer selects the negative input of the analog comparator. When this bit is written logic zero, AIN1 is applied to the negative input of the analog comparator.

The ADMUX register is shown in Figure 9-10. MUX2...0 bits are used in Table 9-1.

23.9.1 ADMUX – ADC Multiplexer Selection Register

Bit	7	6	5	4	3	2	1	0	
(0x7C)	REFS1	REFS0	ADLAR	–	MUX3	MUX2	MUX1	MUX0	ADMUX
Read/Write	R/W	R/W	R/W	R	R/W	R/W	R/W	R/W	
Initial Value	0	0	0	0	0	0	0	0	

Figure 9-10. *Bits of the ADMUX register*

The ACSR register is shown in Figure 9-11.

22.3.2 ACSR – Analog Comparator Control and Status Register

Bit	7	6	5	4	3	2	1	0	
0x30 (0x50)	ACD	ACBG	ACO	ACI	ACIE	ACIC	ACIS1	ACIS0	ACSR
Read/Write	R/W	R/W	R	R/W	R/W	R/W	R/W	R/W	
Initial Value	0	0	N/A	0	0	0	0	0	

Figure 9-11. Bits of the ACSR register

ACD bit (Analog Comparator Disable): When this bit is set by writing 1, the analog comparator is switched off.

ACBG bit (Analog Comparator Bandgap Select): When this bit is set, a fixed bandgap reference voltage replaces the positive input to the analog comparator. When this bit is cleared, AIN0 is applied to the positive input of the analog comparator.

ACO bit (Analog Comparator Output): The output of the analog comparator is synchronized and then directly connected to ACO. The synchronization introduces a delay of one to two clock cycles. To check the output of the analog comparator, one can read the ACO bit.

ACI bit (Analog Comparator Interrupt Flag): This bit is set by hardware when a comparator output event triggers the interrupt mode defined by ACIS1 and ACIS0. The analog comparator interrupt routine is executed if the ACIE bit is set and the I-bit in SREG is set. ACI is cleared by hardware when executing the corresponding interrupt handling vector. Alternatively, ACI is cleared by writing a logic one to the flag.

ACIE bit (Analog Comparator Interrupt Enable): When the ACIE bit is written logic one and the I-bit in the status register is set, the analog comparator interrupt is activated. When written logic zero, the interrupt is disabled.

ACIC bit (Analog Comparator Input Capture Enable): When written logic one, this bit enables the input capture function in Timer/Counter1 to be triggered by the analog comparator.

ACIS1 and ACIS0 bits (Analog Comparator Interrupt Mode Select):
These bits determine which comparator events trigger the analog
comparator interrupt. The different settings are shown in Table 9-2.

Table 9-2. *Determining the interrupt mode*

Table 22-2.   ACIS1/ACIS0 Settings

ACIS1	ACIS0	Interrupt Mode
0	0	Comparator interrupt on output toggle.
0	1	Reserved
1	0	Comparator interrupt on falling output edge.
1	1	Comparator interrupt on rising output edge.

When changing the ACIS1/ACIS0 bits, the analog comparator interrupt
must be disabled by clearing its interrupt enable bit in the ACSR register.
Otherwise an interrupt can occur when the bits are changed.

The SREG register is shown in Figure 9-12.

6.3.1   SREG – AVR Status Register

The AVR status register – SREG – is defined as:

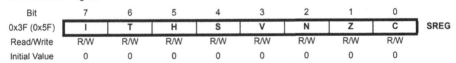

Bit	7	6	5	4	3	2	1	0	
0x3F (0x5F)	I	T	H	S	V	N	Z	C	SREG
Read/Write	R/W	R/W	R/W	R/W	R/W	R/W	R/W	R/W	
Initial Value	0	0	0	0	0	0	0	0	

Figure 9-12. *Bits of the SREG register*

I-bit (Global Interrupt Enable): The global interrupt enable bit must be
set for the interrupts to be enabled. The individual interrupt enable control
is then performed in separate control registers. If the global interrupt
enable register is cleared, none of the interrupts are enabled independent
of the individual interrupt enable settings. The I-bit is cleared by hardware

after an interrupt has occurred and is set by the RETI instruction to enable subsequent interrupts. The I-bit can also be set and cleared by the application with the SEI and CLI instructions, as described in the instruction set reference.

9.10 Example Code for the Internal Comparator

Let's study some example code to see how an internal comparator can be used.

Example 1: Upload the following code to your Arduino board. This code compares two voltages given to pins 6 (PD6) and 7 (PD7). Pins 6 and 7 are connected to + and – terminals of the internal comparator. When the voltage of pin 6 is bigger than pin 7, the onboard LED turns on.

```
/*pin 6 of arduino UNO (+ of comparator) to center terminal of
potentiometer.
 *pin 7 of arduino (- of comparator) to 3.3 V.
*/

void setup() {
  // put your setup code here, to run once:
  ACSR=0x00;    //clear bits of ACSR register
  ADCSRB=0x00;  //clear bits of ADCSRB register

  pinMode(LED_BUILTIN,OUTPUT);
  Serial.begin(9600);
}

void loop() {
  // put your main code here, to run repeatedly:

  // when output of comparator is low, i.e., 0, ACSR&0x20
     generates 0.
```

```
// when output of comparator is high, i.e., 1, ACSR&0x20
   generates 32.
if ((ACSR&0x20)==0){
  digitalWrite(LED_BUILTIN,LOW);
}else{
  digitalWrite(LED_BUILTIN,HIGH);
  }
}
```

The hardware of this example is shown in Figure 9-13. VCC shows the + 5 V pin of the Arduino.

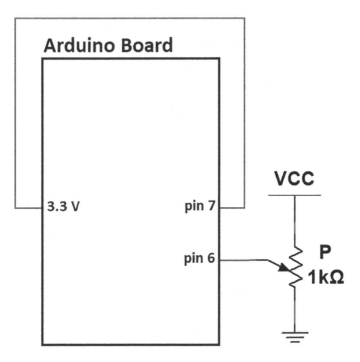

Figure 9-13. *Hardware of the studied example*

Example 2: In this example, the + terminal of the comparator is connected to the internal 1.1 V reference voltage. The negative terminal of the comparator is connected to pin 7 (PD7). The onboard LED turns on

when the voltage applied to pin 7 is less than 1.1 V, and it turns off when
the input voltage is bigger than 1.1 V.

```
/* + terminal of comparator is connected to reference voltage
of 1.1 V.
- terminal is connected to pin 7. center terminal of
  potentiometer is connected to pin 7, as well.
When input voltage is bigger than 1.1 V, onboard LED is off.
When input voltage is less than 1.1 V, onboard LED is on.
*/

void setup() {
  // put your setup code here, to run once:
  ACSR=0b01000000; //makes ACBG=1 which connect the +
                       terminal of the
                   //comparator to internal reference
                       voltage source.
  ADCSRB=0x00;      //clear bits of ADCSRB register

  pinMode(LED_BUILTIN,OUTPUT);
  Serial.begin(9600);
}

void loop() {
  // put your main code here, to run repeatedly:

  // when output of comparator is low, i.e., 0, ACSR&0x20
     generates 0.
  // when output of comparator is high, i.e., 1, ACSR&0x20
     generates 32.
  if ((ACSR&0x20)==0){
    digitalWrite(LED_BUILTIN,HIGH);
  }else{
```

```
    digitalWrite(LED_BUILTIN,LOW);
  }
}
```

The hardware of this example is shown in Figure 9-14. VCC shows the + 5 V pin of the Arduino.

Arduino Board

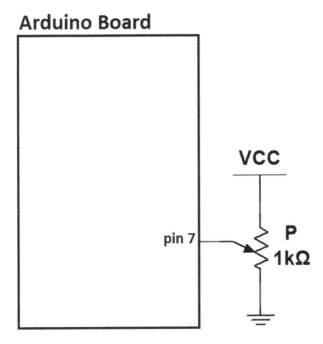

Figure 9-14. *Hardware of the studied example*

Example 3: In this example, the + terminal of the comparator is connected to the reference voltage of 1.1 V. The negative terminal of the comparator is connected to pin A0. The result of the comparison is a suitable string, which is shown in the Serial Monitor.

```
/* + terminal of comparator is connected to reference voltage
of 1.1 V.
- terminal is connected to pin A0 when ADMUX=0 and it is
connected to A1
```

```
when ADMUX=1.
*/

void setup() {
  // put your setup code here, to run once:
  ACSR=0b01000000; //makes ACBG=1 which connect the +
                      terminal of the
                   //comparator to internal reference
                   voltage source.
  ADCSRA=0b00000000;      //ADEN=0.
  ADCSRB=0b01000000;      //ACME=1

  Serial.begin(9600);
}

void loop() {
  // put your main code here, to run repeatedly:
  // when output of comparator is low, i.e., 0, ACSR&0x20
     generates 0.
  // when output of comparator is high, i.e., 1, ACSR&0x20
     generates 32.

  ADMUX=0;  //select A0 for - terminal of comparator
            // ADMUX= 2 selects A2; ADMUX=3 selects A3,...

  if ((ACSR&0x20)==0){
    Serial.println("voltage of A0 is bigger than 1.1 V.");
  }else{
    Serial.println("voltage of A0 is less than 1.1 V.");
  }

  ADMUX=1;  //select A1 for - terminal of comparator
  if ((ACSR&0x20)==0){
    Serial.println("voltage of A1 is bigger than 1.1 V.");
```

```
}else{
   Serial.println("voltage of A1 is less than 1.1 V.");
}

Serial.println("----------------------------------");
delay(2000);
}
```

The hardware of this example is shown in Figure 9-15.

Arduino Board

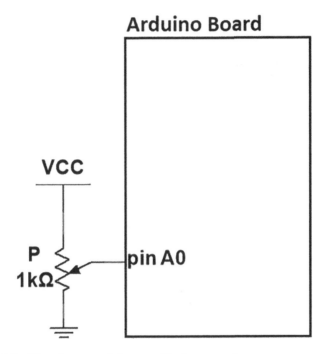

Figure 9-15. *Hardware of the studied example*

Open the Serial Monitor to see the output of the code. You can use a digital voltmeter to measure the voltage of pin A0 and ensure that the output of the code (i.e., shown message) is correct.

Example 4: In this example, we will use the analog comparator interrupt to process the output of the comparison. In this example, the + terminal of the comparator is connected to the 1.1 V internal reference voltage, and the – terminal is connected to analog pin A0. In this example, ANALOG_COMP_vect is called when the result of the comparison goes from low to high, that is, on a rising edge. Note that the name of ISR must be ANALOG_COMP_vect. The onboard LED shows the status of the output of the comparator.

```
/* + terminal of comparator is connected to reference voltage
of 1.1 V.
- terminal is connected to pin A0. Interrupt is used here
  process the output of the output of the comparator.
*/
volatile int n=0;

void setup() {
  // put your setup code here, to run once:
  cli();
  ACSR=0b01001011;    //makes ACBG=1 which connect the +
                        terminal of the
                      //comparator to internal reference
                        voltage source.
                      //set interrupt on rising edge

  ADCSRA=0b00000000;  //ADEN=0.
  ADCSRB=0b01000000;  //ACME=1.
  ADMUX=0;            //select A0 for - terminal of comparator.
  sei();

  pinMode(LED_BUILTIN,OUTPUT);
  Serial.begin(9600);
}
```

```
void loop() {
  // put your main code here, to run repeatedly:
  Serial.println(n);
  digitalWrite(LED_BUILTIN,ACSR&0b00100000);
  //shows the output of the comparator.
  //when led is on output of the comparator is high.
  //when led is off output of the comparator is low.
}

ISR (ANALOG_COMP_vect){
  n++;
}
```

The hardware of this example is shown in Figure 9-16. When the push button is not pressed, 3.3 V reaches analog pin A0. When the push button is pressed, the voltage of pin A0 decreases to 0 V. Therefore, you can apply a voltage above 1.1 V and below 1.1 V to the circuit in order to test it.

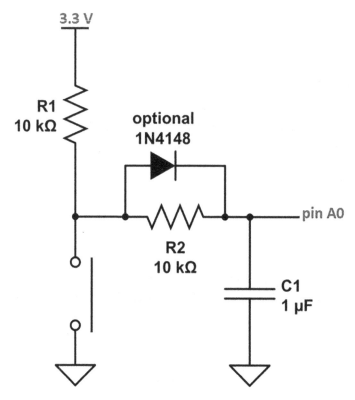

Figure 9-16. *Hardware of the studied example*

Open the Serial Monitor to see the value of variable n. When does the value of variable n change – when the push button is pressed or when it is released? Why?

Example 5: This example is quite similar to the previous example. In this example, the + terminal of the comparator is connected to the 1.1 V internal reference voltage, and the – terminal is connected to analog pin A0. In this example, ANALOG_COMP_vect is called when the result of the comparison goes from high to low, that is, on a falling edge. The onboard LED shows the status of the output of the comparator.

```
/* + terminal of comparator is connected to reference voltage
of 1.1 V.
- terminal is connected to pin A0. Interrupt is used here
process the output of the output of the comparator.
*/
volatile int n=0;

void setup() {
  // put your setup code here, to run once:
  cli();
  ACSR=0b01001010;      //makes ACBG=1 which connect the +
                          terminal of the
                        //comparator to internal reference
                          voltage source.
                        //set interrupt on falling edge

  ADCSRA=0b00000000;  //ADEN=0.
  ADCSRB=0b01000000;  //ACME=1.
  ADMUX=0;            //select A0 for - terminal of comparator.
  sei();

  pinMode(LED_BUILTIN,OUTPUT);
  Serial.begin(9600);
}

void loop() {
  // put your main code here, to run repeatedly:
  Serial.println(n);
  digitalWrite(LED_BUILTIN,ACSR&0b00100000);
  //shows the output of the comparator.
  //when led is on output of the comparator is high.
  //when led is off output of the comparator is low.
}
```

```
ISR (ANALOG_COMP_vect){
  n++;
}
```

The hardware of this example is shown in Figure 9-17. When the push button is not pressed, 3.3 V reaches analog pin A0. When the push button is pressed, the voltage of pin A0 decreases to 0 V. Therefore, you can apply a voltage above 1.1 V and below 1.1 V to the circuit in order to test it.

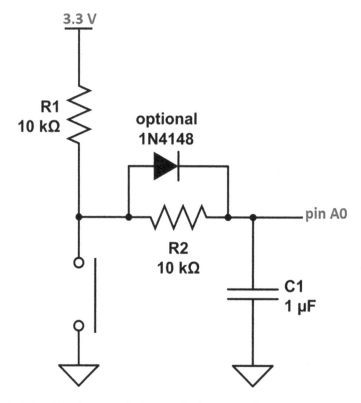

Figure 9-17. *Hardware of the studied example*

Open the Serial Monitor to see the value of variable n. When does the value of variable n change – when the push button is pressed or when it is released? Why?

Example 6: This example is quite similar to the previous two examples. However, calling the ISR happens on both rising (i.e., when the output goes from low to high) and falling edges (i.e., when the output goes from high to low).

```
/* + terminal of comparator is connected to reference voltage
of 1.1 V.
- terminal is connected to pin A0. Interrupt is used here
  process the output of the output of the comparator.
*/
volatile int n=0;

void setup() {
  // put your setup code here, to run once:
  cli();
  ACSR=0b01001000;      //makes ACBG=1 which connect the +
                          terminal of the
                        //comparator to internal reference
                          voltage source.
                        //set interrupt on toggle

  ADCSRA=0b00000000;  //ADEN=0.
  ADCSRB=0b01000000;  //ACME=1.
  ADMUX=0;            //select A0 for - terminal of comparator.
  sei();

  pinMode(LED_BUILTIN,OUTPUT);
  Serial.begin(9600);
}

void loop() {
  // put your main code here, to run repeatedly:
  Serial.println(n);
```

```
  digitalWrite(LED_BUILTIN,ACSR&0b00100000);
  //shows the output of the comparator.
  //when led is on output of the comparator is high.
  //when led is off output of the comparator is low.
}

ISR (ANALOG_COMP_vect){
  n++;
}
```

The hardware of this example is shown in Figure 9-18. When the push button is not pressed, 3.3 V reaches analog pin A0. When the push button is pressed, the voltage of pin A0 decreases to 0 V. Therefore, you can apply a voltage above 1.1 V and below 1.1 V to the circuit in order to test it.

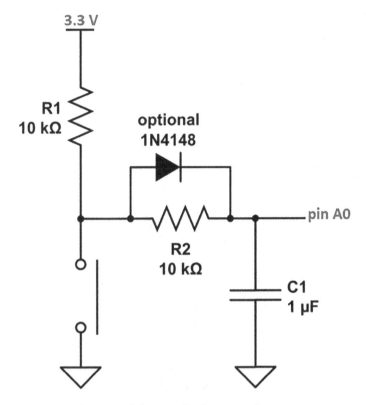

Figure 9-18. *Hardware of the studied example*

Open the Serial Monitor to see the value of variable n. When does the value of variable n change – when the push button is pressed or when it is released? Why?

9.11 Pin Change Interrupt

Arduino UNO has two hardware interrupt pins (pins 2 and 3). Pin change interrupts are another form of a hardware interrupt. Pin change interrupts are restricted, as their name might imply, to only monitoring a change of logic state. So a switch press will generate two interrupts, one when the switch is pressed and a second one when it is released. If you need to know if the interrupt was caused by a HIGH or LOW input, then you'll have to figure that out yourself.

The catch is that pin change interrupts are grouped into ports (port B=pins 8, 9, 10, 11, 12, and 13 of Arduino UNO, port C=pins A0, A1, A2, A3, A4, and A5 of Arduino UNO, and port D=pins 0, 1, 2, 3, 4, 5, 6, 7, and 8 of Arduino UNO), and all the pins on the same port create the same pin change interrupt. This is fine if you are only using one; otherwise, you'll need to figure out which pin caused the interrupt.

Arduino UNO has 24 pin change interrupts (Figure 9-19).

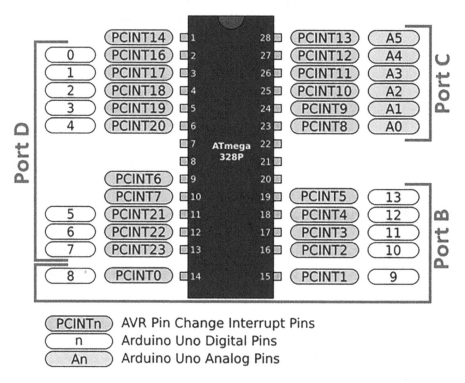

Figure 9-19. *Pin change interrupts assigned to each pin*

The PCICR register (Figure 9-20) is used to enable the pin change interrupt. PCIE0=1 activates the pin change interrupt for pins 8, 9, 10, 11, 12, and 13 of Arduino UNO. PCIE1=1 activates the pin change interrupt for pins A0, A1, A2, A3, A4, and A5 of Arduino UNO. PCIE2=1 activates the pin change interrupt for pins 0, 1, 2, 3, 4, 5, 6, 7, and 8 of Arduino UNO.

12.2.4 PCICR – Pin Change Interrupt Control Register

Bit	7	6	5	4	3	2	1	0	
(0x68)	–	–	–	–	–	PCIE2	PCIE1	PCIE0	PCICR
Read/Write	R	R	R	R	R	R/W	R/W	R/W	
Initial Value	0	0	0	0	0	0	0	0	

Figure 9-20. *Bits of the PCICR register*

PCMSK0, PCMSK1, and PCMSK2 (Figure 9-21) are used to activate the pin change interrupt for the pin(s) that you want.

.

12.2.6 PCMSK2 – Pin Change Mask Register 2

Bit	7	6	5	4	3	2	1	0	
(0x6D)	PCINT23	PCINT22	PCINT21	PCINT20	PCINT19	PCINT18	PCINT17	PCINT16	PCMSK2
Read/Write	R/W	R/W	R/W	R/W	R/W	R/W	R/W	R/W	
Initial Value	0	0	0	0	0	0	0	0	

12.2.7 PCMSK1 – Pin Change Mask Register 1

Bit	7	6	5	4	3	2	1	0	
(0x6C)	–	PCINT14	PCINT13	PCINT12	PCINT11	PCINT10	PCINT9	PCINT8	PCMSK1
Read/Write	R	R/W	R/W	R/W	R/W	R/W	R/W	R/W	
Initial Value	0	0	0	0	0	0	0	0	

12.2.8 PCMSK0 – Pin Change Mask Register 0

Bit	7	6	5	4	3	2	1	0	
(0x6B)	PCINT7	PCINT6	PCINT5	PCINT4	PCINT3	PCINT2	PCINT1	PCINT0	PCMSK0
Read/Write	R/W	R/W	R/W	R/W	R/W	R/W	R/W	R/W	
Initial Value	0	0	0	0	0	0	0	0	

Figure 9-21. *Bits of PCMSK0, PCMSK1, and PCMSK2 registers*

Interrupt service routing for the pin change interrupt must have the following names:

ISR (PCIN0_vect): ISR for port B (pins 8, 9, 10, 11, 12, and 13)

ISR (PCIN1_vect): ISR for port C (pins A0, A1, A2, A3, A4, and A5)

ISR (PCIN2_vect): ISR for port D (pins 0, 1, 2, 3, 4, 5, 6, 7, and 8)

Let's study an example. The following code activates the pin change interrupt of pins 11 and 12. The onboard LED of the board toggles when the user presses or releases the push button connected to these pins.

```
volatile bool state=false;

void setup() {
  // put your setup code here, to run once:
  PCICR|=0b00000001;  // PCINT for pins 8, 9, 10, 11, 12 and 13
                         is enabled.
  PCMSK0|=0b00011000; // Select PCINT3 and PCINT4 = pins 11 and
                         12 of Arduino UNO

  pinMode(LED_BUILTIN,OUTPUT);
  pinMode(11,INPUT_PULLUP);
  pinMode(12,INPUT_PULLUP);
}

void loop() {
  // put your main code here, to run repeatedly:

}
```

```
ISR (PCINT0_vect){
  state=!state;
  digitalWrite(LED_BUILTIN, state);
}
```

The hardware of this example is shown in Figure 9-22.

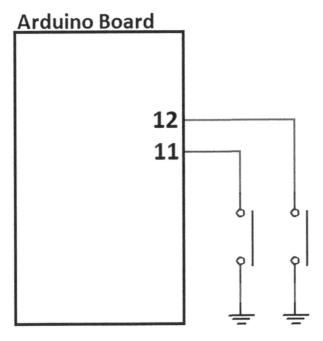

Figure 9-22. Hardware of this example

In the previous code, pressing and releasing of either of the buttons toggle the LED. In other words, there is no difference between the two buttons. Let's change the code to give different functions to each button.

In the following code, pressing the button connected to pin 11 turns on the onboard LED, and pressing the button connected to pin 12 turns off the onboard LED (pay attention to the digitalRead commands inside the ISR). Releasing the buttons has no effect on the status of the onboard LED. The hardware of this example is the same as Figure 9-22.

```
void setup() {
  // put your setup code here, to run once:
  PCICR|=0b00000001;  // PCINT for pins 8, 9, 10, 11, 12 and 13
                         is enabled.
  PCMSK0|=0b00011000; // Select PCINT3 and PCINT4, pins 11 and
                         12 of Arduino UNO

  pinMode(LED_BUILTIN,OUTPUT);
  pinMode(11,INPUT_PULLUP);
  pinMode(12,INPUT_PULLUP);
}

void loop() {
  // put your main code here, to run repeatedly:

}

ISR (PCINT0_vect){
  if (digitalRead(11)==LOW)
    digitalWrite(LED_BUILTIN, LOW);

  if (digitalRead(12)==LOW)
    digitalWrite(LED_BUILTIN, HIGH);
}
```

9.12 References for Further Study

[1]   ATmega328 datasheet:

https://bit.ly/3YKsLn7

[2]   Arduino interrupts:

https://bit.ly/2NdzU9e

[3]   Internal comparator of ATmega328:

https://bit.ly/3jlANCq

https://bit.ly/3PQR3rq

https://bit.ly/3C53YAq

[4]   Arduino interrupts:

https://bit.ly/3YJpMeB

https://bit.ly/3hQThdI

https://bit.ly/2NdzU9e

https://bit.ly/3VynEUg

[5]   RLC meter with Arduino:

https://bit.ly/3Z1ldMS

CHAPTER 10

Timers

10.1 Introduction

A timer or, to be more precise, a timer/counter is a piece of hardware built in the Arduino board's microcontroller. It is like a clock and can be used to measure time events. The timer can be programmed by some special registers. This chapter focuses on the timers and how to use them.

Arduino UNO has three timers: Timer 0, Timer 1, and Timer 2. Timer 0 and Timer 2 are 8-bit counters (they count from 0 to 255), while Timer 1 is a 16-bit counter (it counts from 0 to 65535). The values of timers/counters are stored in the TCNTn register where n=0, 1, and 2. For example, TCNT0 keeps the current value of Timer 0.

Internally, Timer 0 is used for the millis() function, and, therefore, it is recommended not to mess with it. You can use Timer 1 and Timer 2 for your custom requirements.

Figures of this chapter are taken from [1]. The label above each figure shows the location of the figure in the original reference.

© Farzin Asadi 2023
F. Asadi, *Essentials of Arduino™ Boards Programming*, Maker Innovations Series,
https://doi.org/10.1007/978-1-4842-9600-4_10

10.2 Clear Timer on Compare Match (CTC) Mode

In this section, we will see how timers can be used in CTC mode. Let's take a look at the structure of ATmega328 timers first. A simplified block diagram of the 8-bit and 16-bit timers/counters is shown in Figures 10-1 and 10-2, respectively. Tn is the period of the external oscillator connected to the microcontroller. In Arduino UNO, a 16 MHz crystal is used. Therefore, Tn is equal to 1/16000000=62 ns. With the aid of a prescaler, you can give a lower frequency to the counter/timer unit. For example, the clock of timer/counter unit (clkTn in Figures 10-1 and 10-2) is 250 kHz when prescaler=64.

Figure 14-1. 8-bit Timer/Counter Block Diagram

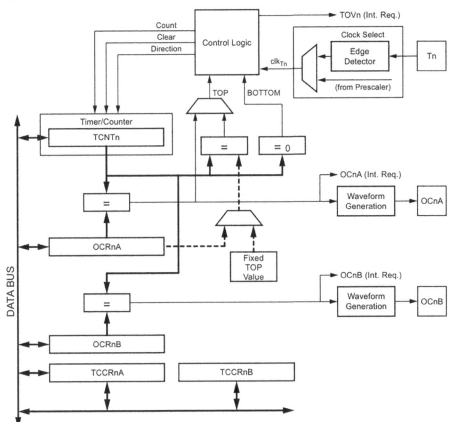

Figure 10-1. *Block diagram of Timer 0 and Timer 2*

Figure 15-1. 16-bit Timer/Counter Block Diagram[1]

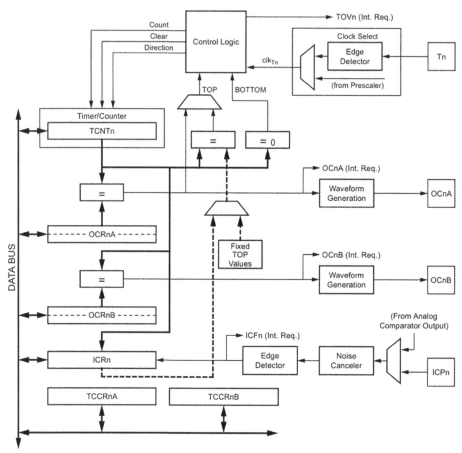

Figure 10-2. *Block diagram of Timer 1*

Study the definitions given in Table 10-1 before going into the details of CTC mode.

Table 10-1. *Bottom, max, and top definitions*

Table 14-1. Definitions

Parameter	Definition
BOTTOM	The counter reaches the BOTTOM when it becomes 0x00.
MAX	The counter reaches its MAXimum when it becomes 0xFF (decimal 255).
TOP	The counter reaches the TOP when it becomes equal to the highest value in the count sequence. The TOP value can be assigned to be the fixed value 0xFF (MAX) or the value stored in the OCR0A register. The assignment is dependent on the mode of operation.

In CTC mode, the timer counts up until the counter value TCNTn (where n is 0, 1, or 2) reaches the TOP value, and at this point, a match occurs and the output at the output compare pin OCnA or OCnB can be either cleared, set, or toggled. The TOP value depends upon which Timer is used. Arduino has three timers called Timer 0, Timer 1, and Timer 2, and each timer can be used in CTC mode. Timer 0 has one CTC mode with TOP at OCR0A, Timer 1 has two CTC modes with TOP at OCR1A and ICR1, and Timer 2 has one CTC mode with TOP at OCR2A.

Let's use Timer 0 for blinking the onboard LED with 1 s durations. Timer 0 registers are shown in Figures 10-3 and 10-4.

14.9.1 TCCR0A – Timer/Counter Control Register A

Bit	7	6	5	4	3	2	1	0	
0x24 (0x44)	COM0A1	COM0A0	COM0B1	COM0B0	–	–	WGM01	WGM00	TCCR0A
Read/Write	R/W	R/W	R/W	R/W	R	R	R/W	R/W	
Initial Value	0	0	0	0	0	0	0	0	

Figure 10-3. *Bits of the TCCR0A register*

14.9.2 TCCR0B – Timer/Counter Control Register B

Bit	7	6	5	4	3	2	1	0	
0x25 (0x45)	FOC0A	FOC0B	–	–	WGM02	CS02	CS01	CS00	TCCR0B
Read/Write	W	W	R	R	R/W	R/W	R/W	R/W	
Initial Value	0	0	0	0	0	0	0	0	

Figure 10-4. *Bits of the TCCR0B register*

293

Descriptions of COM0A1, COM0A0, COM0B1, and COM0B0 bits are given in Tables 10-2 and 10-3.

Table 10-2. *COM0A1 and COM0A0 bit description*

Table 14-2.   Compare Output Mode, non-PWM Mode

COM0A1	COM0A0	Description
0	0	Normal port operation, OC0A disconnected.
0	1	Toggle OC0A on compare match
1	0	Clear OC0A on compare match
1	1	Set OC0A on compare match

Table 10-3. *COM0B1 and COM0B0 bit description*

Table 14-5.   Compare Output Mode, non-PWM Mode

COM0B1	COM0B0	Description
0	0	Normal port operation, OC0B disconnected.
0	1	Toggle OC0B on compare match
1	0	Clear OC0B on compare match
1	1	Set OC0B on compare match

In order to select CTC mode for Timer 0, WGM02, WGM01, and WGM00 must be set to 0, 1, and 0, respectively (mode 2 in Table 10-4).

Table 10-4. *WGM02, WGM01, and WGM00 bit description*

Table 14-8.   Waveform Generation Mode Bit Description

Mode	WGM02	WGM01	WGM00	Timer/Counter Mode of Operation	TOP	Update of OCRx at	TOV Flag Set on[1][2]
0	0	0	0	Normal	0xFF	Immediate	MAX
1	0	0	1	PWM, phase correct	0xFF	TOP	BOTTOM
2	0	1	0	CTC	OCRA	Immediate	MAX
3	0	1	1	Fast PWM	0xFF	BOTTOM	MAX
4	1	0	0	Reserved	–	–	–
5	1	0	1	PWM, phase correct	OCRA	TOP	BOTTOM
6	1	1	0	Reserved	–	–	–
7	1	1	1	Fast PWM	OCRA	BOTTOM	TOP

Notes: 1.   MAX   = 0xFF

2.   BOTTOM = 0x00

Table 10-5 shows how to select the desired prescaler for Timer 0. The value of clkI/O is 16 MHz for Arduino UNO.

Table 10-5. *CS02, CS01, and CS00 bit description*

Table 14-9.   Clock Select Bit Description

CS02	CS01	CS00	Description
0	0	0	No clock source (Timer/Counter stopped)
0	0	1	$clk_{I/O}$ (no prescaling)
0	1	0	$clk_{I/O}$/8 (from prescaler)
0	1	1	$clk_{I/O}$/64 (from prescaler)
1	0	0	$clk_{I/O}$/256 (from prescaler)
1	0	1	$clk_{I/O}$/1024 (from prescaler)
1	1	0	External clock source on T0 pin. Clock on falling edge.
1	1	1	External clock source on T0 pin. Clock on rising edge.

Now the value of OCR is set to $\left[\dfrac{clk_{I/O}}{Presaler}.Desired\ time\ is\ seconds\right]-1.$

For example, when the desired time is 1 ms and prescaler is 64,

OCR= $\dfrac{16\times10^6}{64}\times10^{-3}-1=249$ or $F9$ in hexadecimal.

The following code sets Timer 0 to CTC mode. The Timer0_COMPA_ vect function is run after each 1 ms. When the timer variable reaches 1000, 1 s is passed and we need to toggle the output.

```
/*
This program turns on and off a LED on pin 13 each 1 second
using an internal timer
*/

int timer=0;
bool state=0;

void setup() {
   //put your setup code here, to run once:
   pinMode(LED_BUILTIN,OUTPUT);

   TCCROA=(1<<WGM01);      //Set the CTC mode
   OCROA=0xF9;             //Value for ORCOA for 1ms. OXF9=249 in
                           decimal.

   TIMSKO|=(1<<OCIEOA);    //Set the interrupt request
   sei();                  //Enable interrupt

   TCCROB|=(1<<CS01);      //Set the prescaler equal to 1/64
   TCCROB|=(1<<CS00);
}
```

```
void loop(){
  //put your main code here, to run repeatedly:
  digitalWrite(LED_BUILTIN,state);
}

ISR(TIMER0_COMPA_vect){     //This is the interrupt request
  timer++;
  if(timer>=1000){
    state=!state;
    timer=0;
  }
}
```

The following code uses Timer 0 to generate a 100 kHz square waveform on pin 6 of Arduino. Note that this time we didn't use any ISR.

```
void setup () {
  //OC0A is connected to pin 6 of Arduino
  pinMode(6, OUTPUT);

  TCCR0A=0;  //Reset Timer 0 control registers
  TCCR0B=0;

  // Load 79 to generate 100 kHz sq.wave
  OCR0A = 79;
  // Toggle OC0A on compare match, mode 2 (CTC),No prescalar,
  Start the timer
  TCCR0A = (1 << COM0A0)|(1<<WGM01); //TCCR0A=01000010
  TCCR0B = (1 << CS00); //TCCR1B=00000001
}

void loop() {

}
```

After uploading the code to the Arduino board, connect an oscilloscope to pin 6 and observe the generated waveform. The following code generates a 100 kHz square wave on pin 5:

```
void setup () {
  //OCOB is connected to pin 5 of Arduino
  pinMode(5, OUTPUT);

  TCCROA=0;   //Reset Timer 0 control registers
  TCCROB=0;

  // Load 79 to generate 100 kHz sq.wave
  OCROA = 79;
  // Toggle OCOB on compare match, mode 2 (CTC),No prescalar,
  Start the timer
  TCCROA = (1 << COMOBO)|(1<<WGMO1); //TCCROA=00010010
  TCCROB = (1 << CSOO); //TCCR1B=00000001
}

void loop() {

}
```

The following code generates a 100 kHz square wave on pins 5 and 6 of Arduino:

```
void setup () {
  //OCOB is connected to pin 5 of Arduino
  //OCOA is connected to pin 6 of Arduino

  pinMode(5, OUTPUT);
  pinMode(6, OUTPUT);

  TCCROA=0;   //Reset Timer 0 control registers
  TCCROB=0;
```

```
// Load 79 to generate 100 kHz sq.wave
OCR0A = 79;
// Toggle OC0A and OC0B on compare match, mode 2 (CTC),No
prescalar, Start the timer
TCCR0A = (1 << COM0A0)|(1 << COM0B0)|(1<<WGM01);
//TCCR0A=01010010
TCCR0B = (1 << CS00); //TCCR1B=00000001
}

void loop() {

}
```

10.3 Timer 1 in CTC Mode

Timer 1 registers are shown in Figures 10-5 and 10-6.

15.11.1 TCCR1A – Timer/Counter1 Control Register A

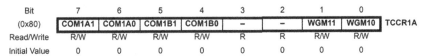

Bit	7	6	5	4	3	2	1	0	
(0x80)	COM1A1	COM1A0	COM1B1	COM1B0	–	–	WGM11	WGM10	TCCR1A
Read/Write	R/W	R/W	R/W	R/W	R	R	R/W	R/W	
Initial Value	0	0	0	0	0	0	0	0	

Figure 10-5. *Bits of the TCCR1A register*

15.11.2 TCCR1B – Timer/Counter1 Control Register B

Bit	7	6	5	4	3	2	1	0	
(0x81)	ICNC1	ICES1	–	WGM13	WGM12	CS12	CS11	CS10	TCCR1B
Read/Write	R/W	R/W	R	R/W	R/W	R/W	R/W	R/W	
Initial Value	0	0	0	0	0	0	0	0	

Figure 10-6. *Bits of the TCCR1B register*

The description of the high nibble of TCCR1A is shown in Table 10-6.

Table 10-6. *COM1A1, COM1A0, COM1B1, and COM1B0 bit description*

Table 15-2.   Compare Output Mode, non-PWM

COM1A1/COM1B1	COM1A0/COM1B0	Description
0	0	Normal port operation, OC1A/OC1B disconnected.
0	1	Toggle OC1A/OC1B on compare match.
1	0	Clear OC1A/OC1B on compare match (set output to low level).
1	1	Set OC1A/OC1B on compare match (set output to high level).

Timer 1 is in the CTC mode when mode 4 or 12 is selected (Table 10-7).

Table 10-7. *WGM13, WGM12, WGM11, and WGM10 bit description*

Table 15-5.   Waveform Generation Mode Bit Description[1]

Mode	WGM13	WGM12 (CTC1)	WGM11 (PWM11)	WGM10 (PWM10)	Timer/Counter Mode of Operation	TOP	Update of OCR1x at	TOV1 Flag Set on
0	0	0	0	0	Normal	0xFFFF	Immediate	MAX
1	0	0	0	1	PWM, phase correct, 8-bit	0x00FF	TOP	BOTTOM
2	0	0	1	0	PWM, phase correct, 9-bit	0x01FF	TOP	BOTTOM
3	0	0	1	1	PWM, phase correct, 10-bit	0x03FF	TOP	BOTTOM
4	0	1	0	0	CTC	OCR1A	Immediate	MAX
5	0	1	0	1	Fast PWM, 8-bit	0x00FF	BOTTOM	TOP
6	0	1	1	0	Fast PWM, 9-bit	0x01FF	BOTTOM	TOP
7	0	1	1	1	Fast PWM, 10-bit	0x03FF	BOTTOM	TOP
8	1	0	0	0	PWM, phase and frequency correct	ICR1	BOTTOM	BOTTOM
9	1	0	0	1	PWM, phase and frequency correct	OCR1A	BOTTOM	BOTTOM
10	1	0	1	0	PWM, phase correct	ICR1	TOP	BOTTOM
11	1	0	1	1	PWM, phase correct	OCR1A	TOP	BOTTOM
12	1	1	0	0	CTC	ICR1	Immediate	MAX
13	1	1	0	1	(Reserved)	–	–	–
14	1	1	1	0	Fast PWM	ICR1	BOTTOM	TOP
15	1	1	1	1	Fast PWM	OCR1A	BOTTOM	TOP

Note: 1.   The CTC1 and PWM11:0 bit definition names are obsolete. Use the WGM12:0 definitions. However, the functionality and location of these bits are compatible with previous versions of the timer.

Table 10-8 shows how to select the desired prescaler for Timer 1. The value of clkI/O is 16 MHz for Arduino UNO.

Table 10-8. *CS12, CS11, and CS10 bit description*

Table 15-6.   Clock Select Bit Description

CS12	CS11	CS10	Description
0	0	0	No clock source (Timer/Counter stopped).
0	0	1	clk$_{I/O}$/1 (no prescaling)
0	1	0	clk$_{I/O}$/8 (from prescaler)
0	1	1	clk$_{I/O}$/64 (from prescaler)
1	0	0	clk$_{I/O}$/256 (from prescaler)
1	0	1	clk$_{I/O}$/1024 (from prescaler)
1	1	0	External clock source on T1 pin. Clock on falling edge.
1	1	1	External clock source on T1 pin. Clock on rising edge.

Let's study an example and see how Timer 1 can be used in CTC mode. The following code generates a 10 kHz square wave on pin 9 of Arduino. This code uses mode 4 (Table 10-7):

```
void setup () {
  //OC1A is connected to pin 9 of Arduino
  pinMode(9, OUTPUT);

  TCCR1A=0; //Reset Timer 1 control registers
  TCCR1B=0;

  // Load 799 to generate 10 kHz sq.wave
  OCR1A = 799;
  // Toggle OC1A on compare match, mode 4 (CTC),No prescalar,
  Start the timer
  TCCR1A = (1 << COM1A0);
  TCCR1B = (1<<WGM12) | (1 << CS10); //TCCR1B=00001001
}

void loop() {

}
```

Connect an oscilloscope to pin 9 of Arduino and ensure that you have a square wave with a frequency of 10 kHz there. The following code generates a 10 kHz square wave on pin 9 of Arduino using mode 12 (Table 10-7):

```
void setup () {
  //OC1A is connected to pin 9 of Arduino
  pinMode(9, OUTPUT);

  TCCR1A=0; //Reset Timer 1 control registers
  TCCR1B=0;

  // Load 799 to generate 10 kHz sq.wave
  ICR1 = 799;
  // Toggle OC1A on compare match, mode 12 (CTC),No prescalar,
  Start the timer
  TCCR1A = (1 << COM1A0);
  TCCR1B = (1<<WGM13) | (1<<WGM12) | (1 << CS10);
  //TCCR1B=00011001
}

void loop() {

}
```

Connect an oscilloscope to pin 9 of Arduino and ensure that you have a square wave with a frequency of 10 kHz there. The following code generates a 10 kHz square wave on pin 10 of Arduino. After uploading the code to the Arduino board, connect an oscilloscope to pin 10 and ensure that you see the 10 kHz square wave on pin 10.

```
void setup () {
  //OC1B is connected to pin 10 of Arduino
  pinMode(10, OUTPUT);

  TCCR1A=0; //Reset Timer 1 control registers
  TCCR1B=0;
```

```
  // Load 799 to generate 10 kHz sq.wave
  ICR1 = 799;
  // Toggle OC1B on compare match, mode 12 (CTC),No prescalar,
  Start the timer
  TCCR1A = (1 << COM1B0);
  TCCR1B = (1<<WGM13) | (1<<WGM12) | (1 << CS10);
  //TCCR1B=00011001
}

void loop() {

}
```

The following code generates the 10 kHz square wave on pins 9 and 10 simultaneously:

```
void setup () {
  //OC1A is connected to pin 9 of Arduino
  //OC1B is connected to pin 10 of Arduino

  TCCR1A=0; //Reset Timer 1 control registers
  TCCR1B=0;

  pinMode(9, OUTPUT);
  pinMode(10, OUTPUT);
  // Load 799 to generate 10 kHz sq.wave
  ICR1 = 799;
  // Toggle OC1A and OC1B on compare match, mode 12 (CTC),No
  prescalar, Start the timer
  TCCR1A = (1 << COM1A0)|(1 << COM1B0);
  TCCR1B = (1<<WGM13) | (1<<WGM12) | (1 << CS10); //TCCR1B=00011001
}

void loop() {

}
```

10.4 Timer 2 in CTC Mode

Timer 2 registers are shown in Figures 10-7 and 10-8.

17.11.1 TCCR2A – Timer/Counter Control Register A

Bit	7	6	5	4	3	2	1	0	
(0xB0)	COM2A1	COM2A0	COM2B1	COM2B0	–	–	WGM21	WGM20	TCCR2A
Read/Write	R/W	R/W	R/W	R/W	R	R	R/W	R/W	
Initial Value	0	0	0	0	0	0	0	0	

***Figure 10-7.** Bits of the TCCR2A register*

17.11.2 TCCR2B – Timer/Counter Control Register B

Bit	7	6	5	4	3	2	1	0	
(0xB1)	FOC2A	FOC2B	–	–	WGM22	CS22	CS21	CS20	TCCR2B
Read/Write	W	W	R	R	R	R	R/W	R/W	
Initial Value	0	0	0	0	0	0	0	0	

***Figure 10-8.** Bits of the TCCR2B register*

The description of the high nibble of TCCR2A is shown in Tables 10-9 and 10-10.

***Table 10-9.** COM2A1 and COM2A0 bit description*

Table 17-2.   Compare Output Mode, non-PWM Mode

COM2A1	COM2A0	Description
0	0	Normal port operation, OC0A disconnected.
0	1	Toggle OC2A on compare match
1	0	Clear OC2A on compare match
1	1	Set OC2A on compare match

Table 10-10. *COM2B1 and COM2B0 bit description*

Table 17-5.   Compare Output Mode, non-PWM Mode

COM2B1	COM2B0	Description
0	0	Normal port operation, OC2B disconnected.
0	1	Toggle OC2B on compare match
1	0	Clear OC2B on compare match
1	1	Set OC2B on compare match

Table 10-11 shows how to select the desired prescaler for Timer 2. The value of clk is 16 MHz for Arduino UNO.

Table 10-11. *CS22, CS21, and CS20 bit description*

Table 17-9.   Clock Select Bit Description

CS22	CS21	CS20	Description
0	0	0	No clock source (Timer/Counter stopped).
0	0	1	clk/(no prescaling)
0	1	0	clk/8 (from prescaler)
0	1	1	clk/32 (from prescaler)
1	0	0	clk/64 (from prescaler)
1	0	1	clk/128 (from prescaler)
1	1	0	clk/256 (from prescaler)
1	1	1	clk/1024 (from prescaler)

Timer 2 is in the CTC mode when mode 2 is selected (Table 10-12).

Table 10-12. *WGM22, WGM21, and WGM20 bit description*

Table 17-8.   Waveform Generation Mode Bit Description

Mode	WGM22	WGM21	WGM20	Timer/Counter Mode of Operation	TOP	Update of OCRx at	TOV Flag Set on[1][2]
0	0	0	0	Normal	0xFF	Immediate	MAX
1	0	0	1	PWM, phase correct	0xFF	TOP	BOTTOM
2	0	1	0	CTC	OCR2A	Immediate	MAX
3	0	1	1	Fast PWM	0xFF	BOTTOM	MAX
4	1	0	0	Reserved	–	–	–
5	1	0	1	PWM, phase correct	OCR2A	TOP	BOTTOM
6	1	1	0	Reserved	–	–	–
7	1	1	1	Fast PWM	OCR2A	BOTTOM	TOP

Notes: 1.   MAX = 0xFF
         2.   BOTTOM = 0x00

The following code generates a 100 kHz square wave on pin 11:

```
void setup () {
  //OC2A is connected to pin 11 of Arduino.
  pinMode(11, OUTPUT);

  TCCR2A=0;  //Reset Timer 2 control registers
  TCCR2B=0;

  // Load 79 to generate 100 kHz sq.wave
  OCR2A = 79;
  // Toggle OC2A on compare match, mode 2 (CTC),No prescalar,
  Start the timer
  TCCR2A = (1 << COM2A0)|(1<<WGM21); //TCCR2A=01000010
  TCCR2B = (1 << CS20); //TCCR2B=00000001
}

void loop() {

}
```

In the following code, ISR is called each 16.38 ms. After uploading the code, open the Serial Monitor to see the output.

```
volatile long i=0;

void setup () {
  TCCR2A=0;   //Reset Timer 2 control registers
  TCCR2B=0;

  OCR2A = 255;

  TIMSK2|=(1<<OCIE2A);   //Set the interrupt request
  sei();                 //Enable interrupt

  // Toggle OC2A on compare match, mode 2 (CTC),No prescalar,
  Start the timer
  TCCR2A = (1<<WGM21); //TCCR2A=00000010
  TCCR2B = (1 << CS22)|(1 << CS21)|(1 << CS20);
  //TCCR1B=00000111

  Serial.begin(9600);
}

void loop() {
  Serial.println(i);
}

ISR(TIMER2_COMPA_vect){    //This is the interrupt request
  i++;
}
```

10.5 References for Further Study

[1]   ATmega328 datasheet:

https://bit.ly/3I5ej30

[2]   Arduino CTC mode programming:

https://bit.ly/3YJqMzn

https://bit.ly/3VtKOGa

CHAPTER 11

Reading Different Sensors with Arduino

11.1 Introduction

This chapter shows how some of the commonly used sensors can be connected to the Arduino board. Many of the sensor producers have ready-to-use Arduino libraries for their products, which simplify the use of sensors considerably. Always search the Internet in order to see whether there is a ready-to-use library for your sensor. This helps you to save your time and energy.

11.2 DHT11 Temperature Sensor

DHT11 can be used to measure temperature (0–50°C) and humidity (20–90% RH). The temperature and humidity accuracy are ±2°C and ±5% RH, respectively. The pinout of this sensor is shown in Figure 11-1. This sensor has an 8-bit microcontroller.

© Farzin Asadi 2023
F. Asadi, *Essentials of Arduino™ Boards Programming*, Maker Innovations Series,
https://doi.org/10.1007/978-1-4842-9600-4_11

Figure 11-1. *DHT11 temperature sensor*

The connection of DHT11 to a typical microcontroller is shown in Figure 11-2. DHT11's power supply is 3–5.5 V DC. When the connecting cable is shorter than 20 meters, a 5 kΩ pull-up resistor is recommended.

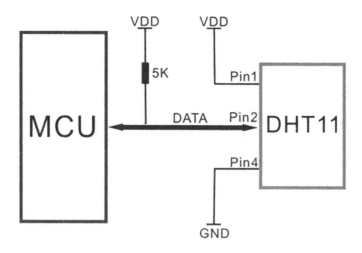

Figure 11-2. *Connection of DHT11 to a microprocessor*

Upload the following code to the Arduino board. Connect the +5 V, GND, and pin 7 of Arduino to pins 1, 4, and 2 of the DHT11 sensor. Open the Serial Monitor to see the output of the code.

```
#include <DHT.h> //DHT Sensor Library: https://github.com/
adafruit/DHT-sensor-library
int DHTPIN=7;
float humidity;
float temperature;
DHT dht(DHTPIN, DHT11);

void setup() {
  Serial.begin(9600);
  dht.begin();
}

void loop() {
  delay(2000);
  humidity = dht.readHumidity();
  temperature= dht.readTemperature();
  Serial.print("Humidity (in %): ");
  Serial.println(humidity);
  Serial.print("Temperature(in C): ");
  Serial.println(temperature);
  Serial.println("--------------------");
}
```

11.3 HCSR04 Ultrasonic Sensor

The HCSR04 module permits you to read the distance using a 40 kHz ultrasonic sound wave. This sensor works with 5 V.

Click Tools ➤ Manage Libraries. This opens the Library Manager window for you. Search for HCSR04 and install the version written by Martin Sosic (Figure 11-3).

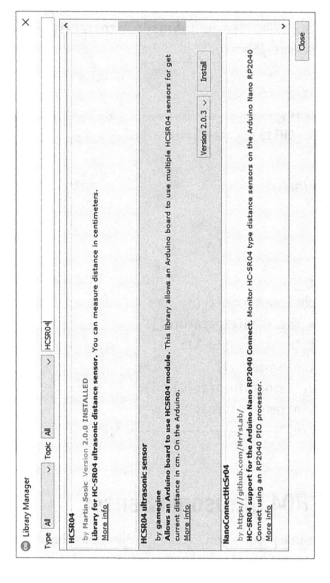

Figure 11-3. Library Manager window

Upload the following code to the board. Connect the VCC, Trig, Echo, and GND pins of the module to the +5 V, 13, 12, and GND pins of the Arduino board. Open the Serial Monitor to see the output of the code.

```
#include <HCSR04.h>

UltraSonicDistanceSensor distanceSensor(13, 12);  // Initialize
sensor that uses digital pins 13(Trig) and 12 (Echo).

void setup () {
    Serial.begin(9600);  // We initialize serial connection so
    that we could print values from sensor.
}

void loop () {
    // Every 500 miliseconds, do a measurement using the sensor
    and print the distance in centimeters.
    Serial.println(distanceSensor.measureDistanceCm());
    delay(500);
}
```

11.4 YL69 Soil Moisture Sensor

YL69 (Figure 11-4) can be used to measure the moisture of soil. You can use this sensor to make an automatic watering system.

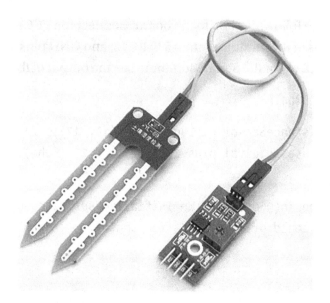

Figure 11-4. *YL69 soil moisture sensor*

Upload the following code to the board. Connect the VCC, GND, and A0 pins of YL69 to +5, GND, and A0 pins of Arduino. Open the Serial Monitor to see the output of the code.

```
//https://randomnerdtutorials.com/guide-for-soil-moisture-
sensor-yl-69-or-hl-69-with-the-arduino/
int analogPin= A0;
int thresholdValue = 800;

void setup(){
  pinMode(analogPin, INPUT);
  Serial.begin(9600);
}

void loop() {
  int sensorValue = analogRead(analogPin);

  Serial.print((String)"Sensor value: "+sensorValue+". ");
```

```
if(sensorValue < thresholdValue){
  Serial.println("Doesn't need watering.");
}else{
  Serial.println("Time to water your plant.");
}

delay(500);
}
```

11.5 References for Further Study

[1]   DHT11 datasheet:

      https://bit.ly/3joL7cR

[2]   HCSR04 datasheet:

      https://bit.ly/3Wmb2AC

[3]   HCSR04 library:

      https://bit.ly/3C4BkiC

[4]   YL69 datasheet:

      https://bit.ly/3GjSXgX

[5]   ADXL3xx accelerometer:

      https://bit.ly/3GlBmp8

[6]   Rotary encoder:

      https://bit.ly/3FWaw5n

APPENDIX A

Testing the Components

A.1 Introduction

Sometimes, you need to test your components to ensure that they are not faulty. This appendix shows how to test some of the most commonly used components.

A.2 Testing the Resistors

You can use a digital multimeter to measure the value of a resistor (Figure A-1). If the value is close to the value shown by the color bands and your measurements are close, then you can deduce that the resistor is good.

© Farzin Asadi 2023

F. Asadi, *Essentials of Arduino™ Boards Programming*, Maker Innovations Series, https://doi.org/10.1007/978-1-4842-9600-4

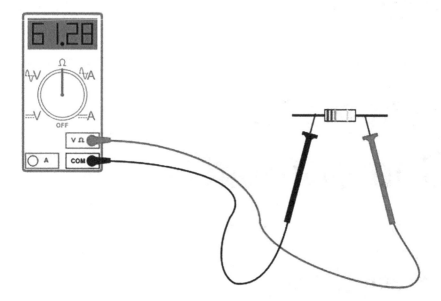

Figure A-1. *Measurement of resistance with digital multimeter*

You need to know the resistance of the probes when you want to measure small resistors (i.e., in the range of a few Ohms). You can measure the probe's resistance by connecting the probes together as shown in Figure A-2. For instance, in Figure A-2 the resistance of the probes is 0.4 Ω. If you connect the probes to a resistor and the digital multimeter shows 2.6 Ω, then the real value is 2.6 –0.4 = 2.2 Ω.

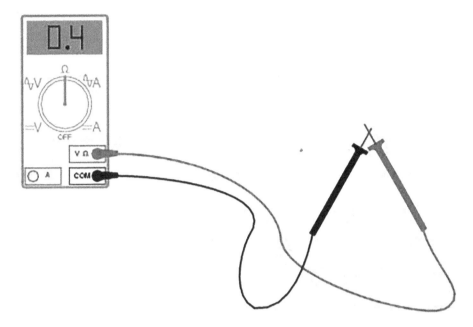

Figure A-2. *Measurement of the probe's resistance*

If you want to measure the resistance of a resistor which is connected to a printed circuit board (PCB), then you need to take out and isolate at least one of its legs. The reason for this could be understood with the aid of the simple circuit shown in Figure A-3. In this circuit, four 10 kΩ resistors are connected in parallel. When you connect the probes directly to the resistor under measurement (the left-hand-side resistor), you will read 2.5 kΩ because other components in the circuit affect your measurement. When you isolate at least one of the legs (Figures A-4 and A-5), you don't permit other elements in the circuit to affect your measurement.

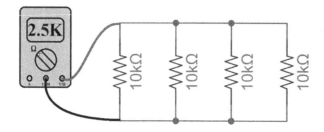

Figure A-3. *A simple parallel circuit*

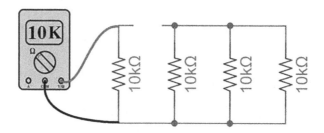

Figure A-4. *One leg of the resistor is isolated from the circuit*

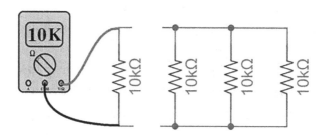

Figure A-5. *Both legs of the resistor are isolated from the circuit*

You can test the transformers and incandescent lamps with the resistance measurement section of the digital multimeter as well (Figure A-6). When the transformer winding is opened, or the lamp is blown, you read infinity (i.e., it shows OL).

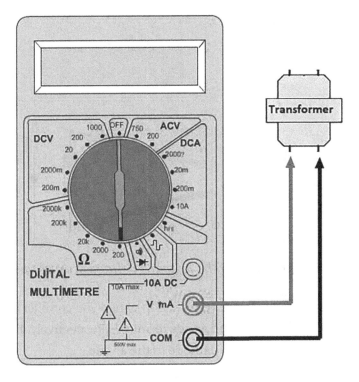

Figure A-6. *Testing a transformer with a digital multimeter*

A.3 Testing the Diodes

You can test the diode by selecting the diode section of the digital multimeter, connecting the red probe to the anode and connecting the black probe to the cathode. The number shown on the display is the forward voltage drop of the diode (Figure A-7).

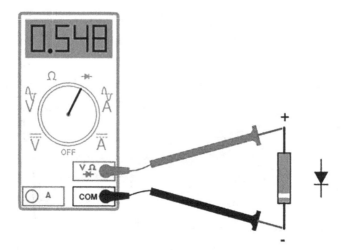

Figure A-7. *Measurement of the forward voltage drop of the diode*

You need to observe the OL (Open Loop) when you connect the red and black probes to cathode and anode terminals, respectively. Remember that no current can go from the cathode to the anode.

A.4 Testing the LEDs

You can test the LEDs with the aid of the circuit shown in Figure A-8. If the LED turns on, you deduce that it is not faulty. The voltage drop of the LED is between 1.8 V and 3.3 V. The voltage drop varies by the color of the LED.

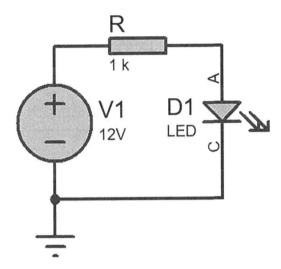

Figure A-8. *Testing the LED*

A.5 Testing the Capacitors and Inductors

You need an LCR meter to measure the capacitance and inductance. Some digital multimeters are able to measure capacitance and inductance as well.

A.6 Servo Motor Tester with 555 IC

A servo motor is a special type of electric motor coupled to a sensor for position feedback. The position of shaft is controllable in this type of motor. Servo motors are widely used in digital cameras, robots, toys (e.g., model cars/aircrafts/boats), etc.

The 555 IC can be used to test small servo motors as well. Circuits shown in Figures A-9 and A-10 can be used for this purpose.

You can rotate the servo motor shaft either in clockwise or counterclockwise directions by pushing the push buttons shown in Figure A-9 or the potentiometer shown in Figure A-10.

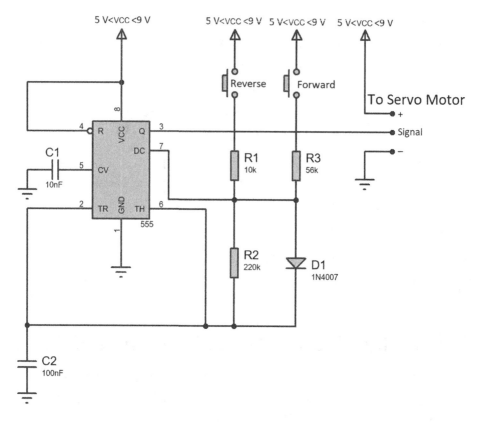

Figure A-9. *The position of the servo motor shaft is controlled with the aid of two push buttons*

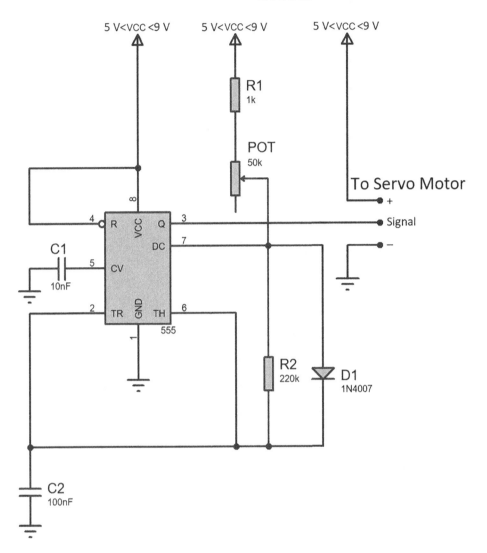

Figure A-10. *The position of the servo motor shaft is controlled with the aid of a potentiometer*

Index

© Farzin Asadi 2023
F. Asadi, *Essentials of Arduino™ Boards Programming*, Maker Innovations Series,
https://doi.org/10.1007/978-1-4842-9600-4

E, F, G

H

I, J, K

Printed in the United States
by Baker & Taylor Publisher Services